from Amy   3/13

THE COURAGE TO BE

SECOND EDITION

THE COURAGE TO BE

PAUL TILLICH

WITH AN INTRODUCTION BY
PETER J. GOMES

YALE UNIVERSITY PRESS
NEW HAVEN & LONDON

For information about this and other Yale University Press publications,
please contact:

    U.S. office   sales.press@yale.edu
    Europe office   sales@yaleup.co.uk
Printed in the United States of America.
Library of Congress Card Number: 00-102364

ISBN 978-0-3000-8471-9
ISBN 0-300-08471-4 (pbk.)

A catalogue record for this book is available from the British Library.

10 9 8 7 6

For René

CONTENTS

Few theologians have been able to capture the imagination of the modern world as Paul Tillich. He was one who, in the middle of the twentieth century, spoke convincingly to the crisis of spirit and mind that hovered over the religious life of thoughtful people. Described by an admirer as the "Apostle to the intellectuals," Tillich, through his many writings—first in German and then in English—provided a new theological vocabulary with which to address the profound disquietude provoked by modernity's confrontation with death and meaninglessness. Admired by his fellow theologians as a "theologian's theologian," he was read by an ever-widening and appreciative circle of lay people for whom much of Christian theology and philosophy had proven itself inaccessible and irrelevant. By creating a new and dynamic theological vocabulary with which to examine the contemporary crisis of anxiety, Tillich liberated theology from the academy and gave it both a new audience and a new relevance in contemporary discourse.

Paulus Johannes Tillich was born in Germany in 1886 and educated at the Universities of Berlin, Tübingen, Halle, and Breslau. Ordained a minister in the Lutheran Church in 1912, he taught theology in universities in

Germany until 1933, when he was deprived by the
Nazis of his professorship. Admired by American col-
leagues, he was invited by Reinhold Niebuhr to teach
at Union Theological Seminary in New York City,
where he remained from 1933 until his appointment in
1955 as University Professor at Harvard. He left Harvard for the University of Chicago in 1962, where he
taught until his death in 1965.

Of all of his many writings, none better captures the
essence of Tillich's thought than *The Courage to Be*,
published in 1952. He had long been well known and
appreciated within the specialized world of theology
and philosophy, but with the publication of this book
he burst upon the wider cultural scene and became
something of an American intellectual celebrity. The
book became an indispensable classic, without which
serious discussion about the meaning of life could not
be undertaken, and it is virtually impossible to think of
another book published in the twentieth century in the
field of religion which had the immediate impact of
The Courage to Be. No college reading list was complete
without it, and its very title entered into the lexicon of
theological conversation.

The book began as a set of lectures given under the
auspices of the Terry Foundation at Yale University.
The terms of the foundation required that the lectures
concern themselves with "religion in the light of science and philosophy," and Tillich chose as his subject
the concept of courage because he was convinced that

it was the place in which theological, sociological, and philosophical problems converged in such a way as to provide a useful analysis of the human situation. "Courage," he wrote in the opening paragraph, "is an ethical reality, but it is rooted in the whole breadth of human existence and ultimately in the structure of being itself. It must be considered ontologically in order to be understood ethically." This was the device with which he would examine modernity's most consuming crisis: meaninglessness and its discontents.

His lectures could not have come at a more paradoxical moment in American culture and religious life. The postwar recovery was well under way, and with it the rise of a cultural optimism in a country which had both won the war and defeated the depression: material prosperity was an ambition and a fact of life. America was now the defender of the free world, and with that fact came a sense of self-satisfaction and security. Religion participated in this boom culture with a marked increase in church attendance and an epidemic of church building programs across the country, which *Time* magazine called America's religious "edifice complex." Billy Graham was filling America's largest public spaces with his crusades, Norman Vincent Peale was perennially on the best-seller list, and Bishop Fulton J. Sheen was almost as popular as comedian Milton Berle in the new leveling medium of television. At Harvard University, the new young president Nathan Marsh Pusey was busily reviving the moribund Divinity School with an infusion of new millions from John D. Rockefeller, Jr., and new and vigorous theologians. Tillich himself would join that faculty in 1955, and on March 16, 1959, his picture would grace the cover of *Time* magazine. Religion was experiencing one of its periodic flourishings in American life and, this time, it appeared to be here to stay.

Tillich, however, was not quite so persuaded of the depth or permanence of America's latest revival of religion. In the middle of the religious boom of the 1950s, in an article entitled "The Lost Dimension in Religion" in the June 14, 1958, issue of the *Saturday Evening Post*, then the most popular magazine in America, Tillich wrote, "If we define religion as the state of being grasped by an infinite concern we must say: man in our time has lost such an infinite concern. And the resurgence of religion is nothing but a desperate and mostly futile attempt to regain what has been lost."[1] Tillich was not easily impressed by expressions of popular piety and the building boom in churches, and it was to the subject of what had been lost, the so-called "lost dimension in religion," to which he turned in *The Courage to Be*.

In our age of intellectual specialization and the marginalization of religion from thoughtful society, and of compelling ideas from much of religion, it is difficult to imagine a theologian being taken seriously by anyone other than other sympathetic theologians. Paul Tillich, however, was taken very seriously by the culture at large, as well as by theologians. The publishers of *Time* and the *Saturday Evening Post* knew what they were doing when they gave over their pages to Tillich, for people were prepared to hear what he had to say even if they did not always understand it. He was, after all, the incarnation of the German "Herr Doktor Professor." Tall and elegantly disheveled, he spoke ponderously and with a heavy German accent, theology's answer, as it were, to science's Albert Einstein: an eminent intellectual who managed to capture the popular imagination.

From his platform as a professor at New York's Union Theological Seminary during the 1930s and 1940s, Tillich gained his reputation as a critical and articulate philosopher of culture, appealing to new audiences across the country eager for more than the popular preaching of the day. As a new generation of teachers of religion and philosophy—who had heard and read him in their own student days—went to fill appointments in America's colleges and seminaries, they introduced their students to the work of Paul Tillich: by mid-century he was a ubiquitous figure on the college lecture circuit and beginning to have an impact.

After the publication of his 1952 Terry Lectures as *The Courage to Be*, Tillich became a genuine intellectual celebrity, with his book appearing on practically every college's reading list. It was the stuff of college bull sessions on religion: preachers and professors borrowed freely from it, and it became what one might call an "iconic" book, that is, a book that everyone has heard of and most felt that they ought to have read. My first en-

counter with it was in my freshman year at Bates
College in 1961, when it appeared on the reading list of
Religion 101. Paul Tillich had been my professor's professor, and he never got over it; an entire theological
generation would feel the same.

When I was invited to prepare this introduction to a
new Yale University Press edition of Tillich's book, I
was delighted. I knew that I had read *The Courage to Be*,
or had at least been examined in it many years ago, but,
truth to tell, I could not remember a thing about it except, of course, the intriguing notion of fortitude and
existence in what has to be one of the best titles ever
for any theological book. I was therefore obliged to
read *The Courage to Be* again, this time with the eyes of
a post-modern apologist for belief in the closing shad-
ows of the twentieth century, and I wondered if I would
find it dated, irrelevant, incomprehensible, or, in short,
a period piece. To my surprise and delight, nothing
could have been further from the case.

At the end of the twentieth century, despite all of the
superficial signs of religious vitality in American life
and culture, where presidential candidates are obliged
to boast of their intimacy with Jesus Christ, the nag-
ging clouds of doubt and meaning continue to rain on
our religious parade. In an era of unprecedented economic growth and material prosperity, where more
people have more faith in the chairman of the Federal
Reserve Bank than in the president of the United
States, there remains at the heart of the culture a grave

and disquieting anxiety. We work hard and play hard not because we are more industrious or more playful than our ancestors but because we dare not stop lest in the stillness we are overwhelmed by the sound of our own anxieties and fears. Standing on the edge of a new century and millennium, seemingly "masters of the universe," in Tom Wolfe's sardonic phrase, we live more in a world in which, as described by George Orwell in his essay "Pleasure Spots":

> The lights must never go out,
> The music must always play,
> Lest we should see where we are—
> Lost in a haunted wood;
> Children afraid of the dark
> Who have never been happy or good.

To this condition of existentialist doubt Tillich spoke, and in the last sentence of the book he both defined his title and offered his solution:

> The courage to be is rooted in the God who appears when God has disappeared in the anxiety of doubt. (190)

Another way of putting this concept is that our only hope is the hope that appears when the situation is beyond hope itself, or hopeless. This complex concept was anticipated in early 1900 by the African American poet James Weldon Johnson, who in his poem/song "Lift Ev'ry Voice and Sing" spoke of the African American's persistent hope "when hope unborn had died."

Religion, for many moderns, had been reduced to a

belief in the unbelievable. Darwin, Freud, and Marx had created a world in which it was now possible, even desirable, so it seemed, to do without the divine hypothesis; and the result was not happiness or freedom but anxiety and bondage to fear. If there was neither a heaven for reward nor a hell for punishment, if God was created in the image of man and not the other way around, then where were meaning and value to be found? If earthly order was neither a replication nor an anticipation of divine order, what good was order at all? In fact, was not order itself in these circumstances of modernity a false god which deserved no deference?

The religious responded to modernity either by trying to accommodate religious belief to its standards of credibility, giving birth to the theological position called 'modernism', or by resisting modernity altogether and appealing with emotional energy and rational argument to adamantly pre-modern fundamentals, the theological position of fundamentalism. The secular, according to Tillich, responded to the same dilemma by creating a collectivist cultural absolute as in communism and fascism, or a conformist cultural absolute as in the American capitalist society of the twentieth century. Much of the intellectual response to the triumph of secular modernism was to be found in the philosophical and cultural position which came to be known as 'existentialism'. Existentialism is a series of philosophical arguments having to do with the relationship between the individual and God or the universe, which have in common a resistance to the metaphysical certainties presupposed by the premodern period in western theology. The fundamental existential question has to do with the fundamental question of individual meaning and purpose in an existence from which God has been displaced as the source of meaning, purpose, and order. Is there, in other words, an alternative to chaos and despair? If there is, how does one—with the will to believe—find it?

This is the problem of the modern situation to which Tillich speaks. He is careful to distinguish three meanings to the term *existentialism*, which he understands to be a content and not simply an attitude: existentialism as point of view, existentialism as protest, and existentialism as expression. As point of view, Tillich argues, existentialism is present in most theology and in much of art, philosophy, and literature. As conscious protest, existentialism appeared in the last third of the nineteenth century and, in Tillich's words, "has largely determined the destiny of the twentieth century. Existentialism as expression is the character of the philosophy, art, and literature of the period of the World Wars and all-pervading anxiety of doubt and meaninglessness. It is the expression of our own situation" (126).

To most Americans who had heard of existentialism in the early 1950s, the very term reeked of the essentially foreign intellectual despondency of postwar Europe where, out of the ruins of Western civilization, there arose the despairing works of Camus and Sartre. Even before the war, brutish civic architecture, the bizarre paintings of Picasso, "modern" poetry that abandoned rhyme and meter, musical atonality, and the general deconstruction of social convention all had manifested themselves as symptoms of a culture not only in transition but in self-mocking despair. The postwar British playwright John Osborne would lead a whole generation of angry young men, and on American television Mort Sahl would make comedy the agency of his own raging cynicism. Existentialism to Tillich, however, was more than simply these instances of the desacrilization of culture. He wrote:

> It [existentialism] is not the invention of a Bohemian philosopher or of a neurotic novelist; it is not a sensational exaggeration made for the sake of profit and fame; it is not a morbid play with negativities. Elements of all these have entered it, but it itself is something else. It is the expression of the anxiety of meaninglessness and of the attempt to take this anxiety into the courage to be as oneself. (139)

By this analysis Tillich was clear that existentialism was not simply a synonym for cynicism. He reminds us that the original Greek cynic was a critic of contemporary culture on the basis of reason and natural law, a revolutionary rationalist, as were the followers of Socrates. Modern cynics rarely follow that high road. They are followers of what he calls "noncreative existentialism," and of them he says that they are not ready to follow anybody and have no belief in reason, no criterion of truth, no set of values, and no answers to the question of meaning. "They try to undermine every norm put before them. . . . They courageously reject any solution which would deprive them of their freedom of rejecting whatever they want to reject." The modern cynic does not contribute to addressing the problem of meaninglessness. "Much compulsive self-affirmation," he argues, "and much fanatical self-surrender are expressions of the noncreative courage to be as oneself" (151).

The courage to be, in the face of existentialism with its temptations to cynical despair and noncreative self-indulgence, is "the courage to accept oneself as accepted in spite of being unacceptable. . . . This is the genuine meaning of the Pauline-Lutheran doctrine of 'justification by faith'" (164). Tillich, unlike most professional theologians, was an able and persuasive preacher, and many people got far more from his sermons than from his formal lectures and writings. One of his most famous and popular sermons, entitled "You are Accepted," expanded upon this aspect of the courage to be. Here he made his famous definition of sin as estrangement or separation and described the human condition as separation from God, from self, and from neighbor. Not only are we aware of our separation, but with all honesty and candor we understand ourselves to deserve that separation. We are unlovely and do not deserve love. Having redefined sin as separation, he proceeds to redefine grace as acceptance:

Grace strikes us when we are in great pain and restlessness.

It strikes us when we walk through the dark valley of a meaningless and empty life. It strikes us when we feel that our separation is deeper than usual, because we have violated another life, a life which we loved, or from which we were estranged.[2]

Then he describes the grace coming to us as a wave of light breaking into our darkness, as if a voice were saying:

You are accepted. You are accepted, accepted by that which is greater than you, and the name of which you do not know. Do not ask for the name now; perhaps you will find it later. Do not try to do anything now; perhaps later you will do much. Do not seek for anything; do not perform anything; do not intend anything. Simply accept the fact that you are accepted! If that happens to us, we experience grace.[3]

In *The Courage to Be*, Tillich describes this as "self-affirmation . . . [which] presupposes participation in something which transcends the self" (165).

Fate, guilt, and the fear of death were the three anxieties that bedeviled the modern spirit. Fate held hostage both meaning and purpose; guilt, in the absence of a source of forgiveness and grace, was a living death; and death, in the absence of meaning in life and with no promise of reward or punishment, was the ultimate experience of meaninglessness. The old theologies and pieties offered certainties which could no longer be sustained in the critical light of modernity, for too much had happened to return to a precritical

age, and too much was at stake to pretend to simplici-
ties in the face of complexities. The circumstances required the courage to readapt and reapply old notions
and concepts to meet the present need, the existential
moment; *The Courage to Be* is filled with such notional
readaptations.

In responding to the anxiety of fate and guilt, for example, Tillich invokes what he calls "the courage of
confidence." Genuine belief is maintained "in spite of"
circumstances that would undermine belief and not
simply because of circumstances that would confirm it.
It does not take a great deal of imagination or courage
to believe that God is on your side when you are pros-
pering or winning; it takes a great deal of courage and
imagination to believe that God is on your side when
you are suffering or losing. To believe in love in the
face of hatred, life in the face of death, day in the dark
of night, good in the face of evil—to some, all of these
may seem to be hopelessly naive, wishful thinking,
"whistling in the dark" (a decidedly non-Tillichian
phrase); but, to Tillich, all of these are manifestations
of enormous courage, the courage of confidence in
more than the sovereignty of fact and appearance.
"Providence," he argues, "is not a theory about some
activities of God; it is the religious symbol of the
courage of confidence with respect to fate and death.
For the courage of confidence says 'in spite of' even to
death" (168). This is the echo of Job, who, in the midst
of his dung hill and despair, gives in to neither and

proclaims, "Though He slay me, yet will I praise Him" (Job 13:15).

Faith is of the same quality. It is neither a theoretical affirmation nor an opinion. It is "the character of accepting acceptance" (172). It is faith that allows grace to do its work, and thus faith no longer is believing in what you know "ain't so," as the old canard has it, nor is it an impossible set of churchly pronouncements. It is the courage to accept the acceptance of the unacceptable: namely, oneself.

In the negative world of denial and death, courage, as Tillich reads it, is the self-affirmation of being in spite of non-being. "The power of this self-affirmation is the power of being which is effective in every act of courage. Faith is the experience of this power" (172).

Absolute faith, for Tillich, is faith in the God above God. This is the ultimate courage, for it takes the radical doubt, the doubt about God, into itself and transcends the theistic idea of God. Modernity has been able to unhorse the god of theism. This has been the theme of much of the late twentieth century's theological discourse, but it was a notion not new to Nietzsche, who anticipated the "God is Dead" theologians of the 1960s. It was not the death of God, however, but the death of the god of theism, or the theistic god, that for Tillich allows the "God above God" to become the ultimate source of the courage to be. It was the concept of the "God above God" which would lead to much confusion.

Contrary to those who argued that Tillich was doing away with God and yielding to modernity's secular atheism, Tillich argued that he was not doing away with God but only with a particular conception of God that could no longer be supported by the honest intellectual inquiry of the modern world. What happens to the God of a prescientific age when that prescientific age itself collapses? The popular anthropomorphic, personal, and mechanistic concepts of God, the "God upstairs," as Bishop John A. T. Robinson would call it in his book *Honest to God*, simply was no longer credible. For Tillich, the collapse of the concept did not imply the collapse of the reality of God; rather, the modern mind must be encouraged to think of the "God above God," that is, of what is above and beyond the limits of our imagination. This "death of God" might lead some to the despair of atheism and meaninglessness, but for Tillich it leads to a greater and deeper faith in a God beyond and above all that we doubt. This new faith is grounded in the God who remains after all other gods have proven themselves inadequate. In other words, there is a God who emerges from the other side of doubt, and from that God we take courage.

This is the God in whom faith, courage, providence, and hope take new meaning, meaning which cannot be undone by the old wars and small victories of modernity. Tillich speaks to this point in "Theism Transcended" (182–186). This is a new manifestation, which he makes all the more clear in his 1958 sermon entitled "Behold, I

Am Doing a New Thing," based on Isaiah 43:16, 18–19.
"The new in history," he writes, "always comes when
people least believe in it. But, certainly, it comes only
in the moment when the old becomes visible as old and
tragic and dying, and when no way out is seen. We live
in such a moment; such a moment is our situation."[4]
The "I" in the text of Isaiah, in Tillich's words, "points
to the source of the really new, to that which is always
old and always new, the Eternal." The God above God
is the Eternal, which is no small claim to make in a
world dejected by the death of theism and obsessed
with its own destruction. "The God above the God of
theism is present, although hidden, in every divine/
human encounter." That is why such encounters are to
be cherished for their potential as manifestations of
that God above God.

From 1955 to 1962, Paul Tillich taught as University
Professor at Harvard, where he was one of the intellectual giants: as University Professor he was at liberty to
teach in any of the faculties. While located in the Divinity School he was not confined to that school, and
he enjoyed an enormous popularity in the Faculty of
Arts and Sciences. A frequent preacher in the Memorial Church, Harvard's chapel, he spoke always to stand-
ing-room-only congregations. While he was described
as a theologian's theologian, that suggested, quite inac-
curately, that only theologians understood him and
that he spoke only to them. In his case it was meant to
suggest that he did the work of theology so splendidly,

so elegantly, and so publicly that he made other theologians admirers of his work and more encouraged in their own.

As a public figure, in many ways Tillich resembled Ralph Waldo Emerson, not so much for the congruence of his ideas with those of the sage of Concord, but rather for his notion of himself as what we would today call a "public intellectual" who was accepted as such by the public. The popularity of public intellectuals was not won at the price of "dumbing down" the complexities of their own thoughts, however, and neither had they much entertainment value; it took work both to listen to and to read them. Most people, however, thought that it was work worthwhile, and they made the effort. In nineteenth-century Concord, for example, it was said that the farmers finished up their afternoon chores early so as to go into town to the Lyceum Hall to hear their neighbor—Emerson—lecture, and when they got home their wives would ask what the lecture was about. A typical reply was, "I don't know, but weren't it grand!" Many of those who sat at Tillich's feet in the Memorial Church, and in countless college chapels and lecture halls across the country, could have said the same thing, but enough of them understood enough of what he was saying to be confronted and impressed with Tillich's analysis of the human condition, of contemporary culture, and with his way of bringing fresh light to old conundrums. American theologian Walter Horton called the popular response to Tillich's thought "respectful mystification."

In 1948, Tillich published a collection of essays drawn from his extensive writings from 1927 to the end of the Second World War. Published by the University of Chicago, the book was called *The Protestant Era*, and beneath the title on the front cover were printed two questions: "What is wrong with Christian civilization?" and "Does Protestantism need a reformation?" Apparently the title originally intended for the book, edited by James Luther Adams of Meadville Theological School, was to have been *The End of the Protestant Era*, but Tillich was advised that such a pessimistic title would not sell well in a postwar culture as robustly Protestant and optimistic as that of the United States. In a concluding essay, "Tillich's Concept of the Protestant Era," Adams employed Friedrich Schleiermacher's famous remark, "The reformation must continue," and suggested that it could very well serve as the epigraph of the writings of Paul Tillich. Neither Tillich nor Schleiermacher espoused a return to sixteenth-century German theology, but as the period of the reformation signaled the end of the age which had preceded it, and the consciousness of which animated those who of necessity provoked change and reform, so too are we living at the end of the age which began with those very reforms. The world is no longer the same place, and it never will be. It is for us to remember that those to whom we look in the past were in fact looking ahead.

The work of the reformation is not to go back to

where our predecessors were, but to persevere on to where they were going. To understand Tillich in his forms as preacher, philosopher, theologian, and critic of culture is of necessity to understand this concept of the continuing reformation, a reformation made all the more essential by the end of the Protestant era brought on by the inevitable forces of humanism and modernity. According to Adams:

> If Protestantism is to play a critical and creative role at this juncture, it must break off certain of its attachments to the outlooks and structures of the cultural epoch that is now approaching its possible dissolution; and it must, through a new understanding and application of its principles, assist in the creation of new forms of integration in church and society.[5]

This call to a new reformation is the subtext of all of Tillich's writings, and it anticipates his adaptive re-use of theological concepts in *The Courage to Be*, which would appear but four years after *The Protestant Era*. Living on the boundary between one age and another was a characteristic intellectual posture for Tillich. It is always a time at risk. In *The Courage to Be*, he warns that Christian theology has a duty and a role to play in such times: "It [theology] should decide for truth against safety, even if the safety is consecrated and supported by the churches" (141). This can place the theologian on the boundary between church and theology as well as between theology and culture, but, for Tillich, to persist in the reformation beyond the Protestant era, to address our systems and our situation, means that he cannot be anywhere else but on the boundary.

As a new student at the Harvard Divinity School in the fall of 1965, I attended, as did nearly everybody else, the memorial service for Paul Tillich, who had died that autumn. There the great and the good spoke their tributes. Of his influence upon the young, President Nathan Marsh Pusey said:

> He saw more clearly than most the predicament of the intelligent, educated, concerned people in the twentieth century who had been cut off from the energies of faith by the cultural orthodoxies of this period. And he wanted more than anything else, deeply and compassionately, to be of help; and he could be of help in this age, and was of help, because artist and philosopher as well as theologian, he cared for culture as well as for Christ.[6]

Tillich's great friend and Harvard colleague, James Luther Adams, wrote of him:

> In his life-long dialogue with past and present, Tillich has sought to do for our time what Augustine attempted in his own desperate age as Rome's sway was foundering in the west: to confront every warring ideology in the hope of freeing a depleted faith of accumulated dross and of renewing the power of religious symbols, so that distracted and alienated spirits might once again be brought to an authentic "ultimate concern" through sharing the faith of a Luther in the New Being in Christ, a faith that knows both the wrath and the love of God, a faith that "justifies" both the intellectual and the moral conscience of man.[7]

In a tribute published by the Divinity School, Robert Neeley Bellah, then a young Harvard associate professor of sociology, wrote, "I was one of those many whom Paul Tillich showed that Christian faith did not have to be 'belief in the unbelievable.' Whether or not I would fit Tillich's or anybody's definition of a Christian I am not sure, but it was Tillich who helped me to see that Jesus as the Christ had something ultimate to do with my life."[8]

Something of the gigantic scope of this philosopher-theologian is compressed in this little book, *The Courage to Be*, and its vitality of thought has not worn thin over time. No one will ever argue that Tillich is an easy afternoon's read. This book does not readily coexist with the easy-reading, low-impact genre of much of contemporary spirituality; it does not lend itself to glib one-liners and inspirational smiley-face notes. The modern dilemma which it describes with profound and insightful acuity has not changed in any positive way since 1952. In fact, one could argue very well that *The Courage to Be* has even more to say at the start of a new century than it had at the mid-point of the last. We are a sadder and somewhat wiser people now than then. We have learned to distrust the easy optimism of Main Street, the blandishments of preachers and politicians who speak only to please. We know that our demons are not easily dismissed, that we yearn for more than simply the ability to get through the day. We would like to make a life and not just a living, which—as we know from our own experience and that of others—takes courage. Tillich does not deny the world in which we find ourselves; he denies the ultimacy of its power over us. Self-affirmation, in the Tillich lexicon, is not an exercise in countering low self-esteem, the kind of ego-boosting so popular in an age which fears failure so much that it refuses to concede that it exists. Self-affirmation, for Tillich, is the paradox of "participation in something which transcends the self" (165).

I cannot imagine a more timely message for a more needy people than that contained in *The Courage to Be*. Its final sentence may well be the beginning of a spiritual adventure for millions of new readers in the new century:

> The courage to be is rooted in the God who appears when God has disappeared in the anxiety of doubt.

PETER J. GOMES

NOTES

1. Quoted in *The Essential Paul Tillich: An Anthology of the Writings of Paul Tillich*, ed. F. Forrester Church (New York: Macmillan, 1987).

2. Ibid., 201.

3. Ibid.

4. Ibid., 279.

5. Paul Tillich, *The Protestant Era*, ed. James Luther Adams (Chicago: University of Chicago Press, 1948), 274.

6. The Memorial Church Archives, Harvard University, Tillich files, Paul Tillich Memorial Service (November 4, 1965).

7. The Memorial Church Archives, Harvard University, Tillich files.

8. Ibid.

THE COURAGE TO BE

CHAPTER 1. *Being and Courage*

In agreement with the stipulation of the Terry Foundation that the lectures shall be concerned with "religion in the light of science and philosophy" I have chosen a concept in which theological, sociological, and philosophical problems converge, the concept of "courage." Few concepts are as useful for the analysis of the human situation. Courage is an ethical reality, but it is rooted in the whole breadth of human existence and ultimately in the structure of being itself. It must be considered ontologically in order to be understood ethically.

This becomes manifest in one of the earliest philosophical discussions of courage, in Plato's dialogue *Laches*. In the course of the dialogue several preliminary definitions are rejected. Then Nikias, the well-known general, tries again. As a military leader he should know what courage is and he should be able to define it. But his definition, like the others, proves to be inadequate. If courage, as he asserts, is the knowledge of "what is to be dreaded and what dared," then the question tends to become universal, for in order to answer it one must have "a knowledge concerning all goods and all evils under all circumstances" (199, C). But this definition contradicts the previous statement that courage is only a part of virtue. "Thus,"

Socrates concludes, "we have failed to discover what courage really is" (199, E). And this failure is quite serious within the frame of Socratic thinking. According to Socrates virtue is knowledge, and ignorance about what courage is makes any action in accordance with the true nature of courage impossible. But this Socratic failure is more important than most of the seemingly successful definitions of courage (even those of Plato himself and of Aristotle). For the failure to find a definition of courage as a virtue among other virtues reveals a basic problem of human existence. It shows that an understanding of courage presupposes an understanding of man and of his world, its structures and values. Only he who knows this knows what to affirm and what to negate. The ethical question of the nature of courage leads inescapably to the ontological question of the nature of being. And the procedure can be reversed. The ontological question of the nature of being can be asked as the ethical question of the nature of courage. Courage can show us what being is, and being can show us what courage is. Therefore the first chapter of this book is about "Being and Courage." Although there is no chance that I shall succeed where Socrates failed, the courage of risking an almost unavoidable failure may help to keep the Socratic problem alive.

COURAGE AND FORTITUDE: FROM PLATO TO THOMAS AQUINAS

The title of this book, *The Courage to Be*, unites both meanings of the concept of courage, the ethical and the ontological. Courage as a human act, as a matter of valuation, is an ethical concept. Courage as the universal and essential self-affirmation of one's being is an ontological concept. The courage to be is the ethical act in which man affirms his own being in spite of those elements of his existence which conflict with his essential self-affirmation.

Looking at the history of Western thought one finds the two meanings of courage indicated almost everywhere, explicitly or implicitly. Since we have to deal in separate chapters with the Stoic and Neo-Stoic ideas of courage I shall restrict myself at this point to the interpretation of courage in the line of thought which leads from Plato to Thomas Aquinas. In Plato's *Republic* courage is related to that element of the soul which is called *thymós* (the spirited, courageous element), and both are related to that level of society which is called *phýlakes* (guardians). Thymós lies between the intellectual and the sensual element in man. It is the unreflective striving toward what is noble. As such it has a central position in the structure of the soul, it bridges the cleavage between reason and desire. At least it could do so. Actually the main trend of Platonic thought and the tradition of Plato's school were dualistic, emphasizing the conflict between the reasonable and the sensual. The bridge was not used. As late as Descartes and Kant, the elimination of the "middle" of man's being (the *thymoeidés*) had ethical and ontological consequences. It was responsible for Kant's moral rigor and Descartes' division of being into thought and extension. The sociological context in which this de-

velopment occurred is well known. The Platonic phýlakes are the armed aristocracy, the representatives of
what is noble and graceful. Out of them the bearers of
wisdom arise, adding wisdom to courage. But this aristocracy and its values disintegrated. The later ancient world
as well as the modern bourgeoisie have lost them; in their
place appear the bearers of enlightened reason and techni-
cally organized and directed masses. But it is remarkable
that Plato himself saw the thymoeidés as an essential function of man's being, an ethical value and sociological quality.

The aristocratic element in the doctrine of courage was
preserved as well as restricted by Aristotle. The motive
for withstanding pain and death courageously is, according to him, that it is noble to do so and base not to do so
(Nic. Eth. iii. 9). The courageous man acts "for the sake
of what is noble, for that is the aim of virtue" (iii. 7).
"Noble," in these and other passages, is the translation
of *kalós* and "base" the translation of *aischrós*, words
which usually are rendered by "beautiful" and "ugly."
A beautiful or noble deed is a deed to be praised. Courage
does what is to be praised and rejects what is to be de-
spised. One praises that in which a being fulfills its potentialities or actualizes its perfections. Courage is the
affirmation of one's essential nature, one's inner aim or
entelechy, but it is an affirmation which has in itself the
character of "in spite of." It includes the possible and, in
some cases, the unavoidable sacrifice of elements which
also belong to one's being but which, if not sacrificed,

would prevent us from reaching our actual fulfillment. This sacrifice may include pleasure, happiness, even one's own existence. In any case it is praiseworthy, because in the act of courage the most essential part of our being prevails against the less essential. It is the beauty and goodness of courage that the good and the beautiful are actualized in it. Therefore it is noble.

Perfection for Aristotle (as well as for Plato) is realized in degrees, natural, personal, and social; and courage as the affirmation of one's essential being is more conspicuous in some of these degrees than in others. Since the greatest test of courage is the readiness to make the greatest sacrifice, the sacrifice of one's life, and since the soldier is required by his profession to be always ready for this sacrifice, the soldier's courage was and somehow remained the outstanding example of courage. The Greek word for courage, *andreía* (manliness) and the Latin word *fortitudo* (strength) indicate the military connotation of courage. As long as the aristocracy was the group which carried arms the aristocratic and the military connotations of courage merged. When the aristocratic tradition disintegrated and courage could be defined as the universal knowledge of what is good and evil, wisdom and courage converged and true courage became distinguished from the soldier's courage. The courage of the dying Socrates was rational-democratic, not heroic-aristocratic.

But the aristocratic line was revived in the early Middle Ages. Courage became again characteristic of nobility. The knight is he who represents courage as a soldier and as a nobleman. He has what was called *hohe Mut*, the high, noble, and courageous spirit. The German language has two words for courageous, *tapfer* and *mutig*. Tapfer originally means firm, weighty, important, pointing to the power of being in the upper strata of feudal society. Mutig is derived from *Mut*, the movement of the soul suggested by the English word "mood." Thus words like *Schwermut*, *Hochmut*, *Kleinmut* (the heavy, the high, the small "spirit"). Mut is a matter of the "heart," the personal center. Therefore mutig can be rendered by *beherzt* (as the French-English "courage" is derived from the French *coeur*, heart). While Mut has preserved this larger sense, *Tapferkeit* became more and more the special virtue of the soldier—who ceased to be identical with the knight and the nobleman. It is obvious that the terms Mut and courage directly introduce the ontological question, while Tapferkeit and fortitude in their present meanings are without such connotations. The title of these lectures could not have been "The Fortitude to Be" (*Die Tapferkeit zum Sein*); it had to read "The Courage to Be" (*Der Mut zum Sein*). These linguistic remarks reveal the medieval situation with respect to the concept of courage, and with it the tension between the heroic-aristocratic ethics of the early Middle Ages on the one hand and on the other the rational-democratic ethics which are a heritage of the Christian-humanistic tradition and again came to the fore at the end of the Middle Ages.

This situation is classically expressed in Thomas Aquinas' doctrine of courage. Thomas realizes and discusses the duality in the meaning of courage. Courage is strength of mind, capable of conquering whatever threatens the attainment of the highest good. It is united with wisdom, the virtue which represents the unity of the four cardinal virtues (the two others being temperance and justice). A keen analysis could show that the four are not of equal standing. Courage, united with wisdom, includes temperance in relation to oneself as well as justice in relation to others. The question then is whether courage or wisdom is the more comprehensive virtue. The answer is dependent on the outcome of the famous discussion about the priority of intellect or will in the essence of being, and consequently, in the human personality. Since Thomas decides unambiguously for the intellect, as a necessary consequence he subordinates courage to wisdom. A decision for the priority of the will would point to a greater, though not a total, independence of courage in its relation to wisdom. The difference between the two lines of thought is decisive for the valuation of "venturing courage" (in religious terms, the "risk of faith"). Under the dominance of wisdom courage is essentially the "strength of mind" which makes obedience to the dictates of reason (or revelation) possible, while venturing courage participates in the creation of wisdom. The obvious danger of the first view is uncreative stagnation, as we find in a good deal of Catholic and some rationalistic thought, while the equally obvious danger of the second view is undirected willfulness, as we find in some Protestant and much Existentialist thinking.

However Thomas also defends the more limited meaning of courage (which he always calls fortitudo) as a virtue beside others. As usual in these discussions he refers to the soldier's courage as the outstanding example of courage in the limited sense. This corresponds to the general tendency of Thomas to combine the aristocratic structure of medieval society with the universalist elements of Christianity and humanism.

Perfect courage is, according to Thomas, a gift of the Divine Spirit. Through the Spirit natural strength of mind is elevated to its supernatural perfection. This however means that it is united with the specifically Christian virtues, faith, hope, and love. Thus a development is visible in which the ontological side of courage is taken into faith (including hope), while the ethical side of courage is taken into love or the principle of ethics. The reception of courage into faith, especially insofar as it implies hope, appears rather early, e.g. in Ambrose's doctrine of courage. He follows the ancient tradition, when he calls fortitudo a "loftier virtue than the rest," although it never appears alone. Courage listens to reason and carries out the intention of the mind. It is the strength of the soul to win victory in ultimate danger, like those martyrs of the Old Testament who are enumerated in Hebrews 11. Courage gives consolation, patience, and experience and becomes indistinguishable from faith and hope.

In the light of this development we can see that every attempt to define courage is confronted with these alternatives: either to use courage as the name for one virtue among others, blending the larger meaning of the word into faith and hope; or to preserve the larger meaning and interpret faith through an analysis of courage. This book follows the second alternative, partly because I believe that "faith" needs such a reinterpretation more than any other religious term.

COURAGE AND WISDOM: THE STOICS

The larger concept of courage which includes an ethical and ontological element becomes immensely effective at the end of the ancient and the beginning of the modern world, in Stoicism and Neo-Stoicism. Both are philosophical schools alongside others, but both are at the same time more than philosophical schools. They are the way in which some of the noblest figures in later antiquity and their followers in modern times have answered the problem of existence and conquered the anxieties of fate and death. Stoicism in this sense is a basic religious attitude, whether it appears in theistic, atheistic, or transtheistic forms.

Therefore it is the only real alternative to Christianity in the Western world. This is a surprising statement in view of the fact that it was Gnosticism and Neoplatonism with which Christianity had to contend on religious-philosophical grounds, and that it was the Roman Empire with which Christianity had to battle on religious-political grounds. The highly educated, individualistic Stoics seem to have been not only not dangerous for the Christians but actually willing to accept elements of Christian theism. But this is a superficial analysis. Christianity had a common basis with the religious syncretism of the ancient world, that is the idea of the descent of a divine being for the salvation of the world. In the religious movements which centered around this idea the anxiety of fate and death was conquered by man's participation in the divine being who had taken fate and death upon himself. Christianity, although adhering to a similar faith, was superior to syncretism in the individual character of the Savior Jesus Christ and in its concrete-historical basis in the Old Testament. Therefore Christianity could assimilate many elements of the religious-philosophical syncretism of the later ancient world without losing its historical foundation; but it could not assimilate the genuine Stoic attitude. This is especially remarkable when we consider the tremendous influence of the Stoic doctrines of the Logos and of the natural moral law on both Christian dogmatics and ethics. But this large reception of Stoic ideas could not bridge the gap between the acceptance of cosmic resignation in Stoicism and the faith in cosmic salvation in Christianity. The victory of the Christian Church pushed Stoicism into an obscurity from which it emerged only in the beginning of the modern period. Neither was the Roman Empire an alternative to Christianity. Here again it is remarkable that among the emperors it was not the willful tyrants of the Nero type or the fanatical reactionaries of the Julian type that were a serious danger to Christianity but the righteous Stoics of the type of Marcus Aurelius. The reason for this is that the Stoic has a social and personal courage which is a real alternative to Christian courage.

Stoic courage is not an invention of the Stoic philosophers. They gave it classical expression in rational terms; but its roots go back to mythological stories, legends of heroic deeds, words of early wisdom, poetry and tragedy, and to centuries of philosophy preceding the rise of Stoicism. One event especially gave the Stoics' courage lasting power—the death of Socrates. That became for the whole ancient world both a fact and a symbol. It showed the human situation in the face of fate and death. It showed a courage which could affirm life because it could affirm death. And it brought a profound change in the traditional meaning of courage. In Socrates the heroic courage of the past was made rational and universal. A democratic idea of courage was created as against the aristocratic idea of it. Soldierly fortitude was transcended by the courage of wisdom. In this form it gave "philosophical consolation" to many people in all sections of the ancient world throughout a period of catastrophes and transformations.

The description of Stoic courage by a man like Seneca shows the interdependence of the fear of death and the fear of life, as well as the interdependence of the courage to die and the courage to live. He points to those who "do not want to live and do not know how to die." He speaks of a *libido moriendi*, the exact Latin term for Freud's "death instinct." He tells of people who feel life as meaningless and superfluous and who, as in the book of Ecclesiastes say: I cannot do anything new, I cannot see anything new! This, according to Seneca, is a consequence of the acceptance of the pleasure principle or, as he calls it, anticipating a recent American phrase, the "good-time" attitude, which he finds especially in the younger generation. As, in Freud, the death instinct is the negative side of the ever-unsatisfied drives of the libido, so, according to Seneca, the acceptance of the pleasure principle necessarily leads to disgust and despair about life. But Seneca knew (as Freud did) that the inability to affirm life does not imply the ability to affirm death. The anxiety of fate and death controls the lives even of those who have lost the will to live. This shows that the Stoic recommendation of suicide is not directed to those who are conquered by life but to those who have conquered life, are able both to live and to die, and can choose freely between them. Suicide as an escape, dictated by fear, contradicts the Stoic courage to be.

The Stoic courage is, in the ontological as well as the moral sense, "courage to be." It is based on the control of reason in man. But reason is not in either the old or the new Stoic what it is in contemporary terminology. Reason, in the Stoic sense, is not the power of "reasoning," i.e. of arguing on the basis of experience and with the tools of ordinary or mathematical logic. Reason for the Stoics is the Logos, the meaningful structure of reality as a whole and of the human mind in particular. "If there is," says Seneca, "no other attribute which belongs to man as man except reason, then reason will be his one good, worth all the rest put together." This means that reason is man's true or essential nature, in comparison with which everything else is accidental. The courage to be is the courage to affirm one's own reasonable nature over against what is accidental in us. It is obvious that reason in this sense points to the person in his center and includes all mental functions. Reasoning as a limited cognitive function, detached from the personal center, never could create courage. One cannot remove anxiety by arguing it away. This is not a recent psychoanalytical discovery; the Stoics, when glorifying reason, knew it as well. They knew that anxiety can be overcome only through the power of universal reason which prevails in the wise man over desires and fears. Stoic courage presupposes the surrender of the personal center to the Logos of being; it is participation in the divine power of reason, transcending the realm of passions and anxieties. The courage to be is the courage to affirm our own rational nature, in spite of everything in us that conflicts with its union with the rational nature of being-itself.

What conflicts with the courage of wisdom is desires and fears. The Stoics developed a profound doctrine of anxiety which also reminds us of recent analyses. They discovered that the object of fear is fear itself. "Nothing," says Seneca, "is terrible in things except fear itself." And Epictetus says, "For it is not death or hardship that is a fearful thing, but the fear of death and hardship." Our anxiety puts frightening masks over all men and things. If we strip them of these masks their own countenance appears and the fear they produce disappears. This is true even of death. Since every day a little of our life is taken from us—since we are dying every day—the final hour when we cease to exist does not of itself bring death; it merely completes the death process. The horrors connected with it are a matter of imagination. They vanish when the mask is taken from the image of death.

It is our uncontrolled desires that create masks and put them over men and things. Freud's theory of the libido is anticipated by Seneca but in a larger context. He distinguishes between natural desires which are limited and those which spring from false opinions and are unlimited. Desire as such is not unlimited. In undistorted nature it is limited by objective needs and is therefore capable of satisfaction. But man's distorted imagination transcends the objective needs ("When astray—your wanderings are limitless") and with them any possible satisfaction. And this, not the desire as such, produces an "unwise (*inconsulta*) tendency toward death."

The affirmation of one's essential being in spite of desires and anxieties creates joy. Lucillus is exhorted by Seneca to make it his business "to learn how to feel joy." It is not the joy of fulfilled desires to which he refers, for real joy is a "severe matter"; it is the happiness of a soul which is "lifted above every circumstance." Joy accompanies the self-affirmation of our essential being in spite of the inhibitions coming from the accidental elements in us. Joy is the emotional expression of the courageous Yes to one's own true being. This combination of courage and joy shows the ontological character of courage most clearly. If courage is interpreted in ethical terms alone, its relation to the joy of self-fulfillment remains hidden. In the ontological act of the self-affirmation of one's essential being courage and joy coincide.

Stoic courage is neither atheistic nor theistic in the technical sense of these words. The problem of how courage is related to the idea of God is asked and answered by the Stoics. But it is answered in such a way that the answer creates more questions than it answers, a fact which shows the existential seriousness of the Stoic doctrine of courage. Seneca makes three statements about the relationship of the courage of wisdom to religion. The first statement is: "Undisturbed by fears and unspoiled by pleasures, we shall be afraid neither of death nor of the gods." In this sentence the gods stands for fate. They are the powers that determine fate and represent the threat of fate. The courage that conquers the anxiety of fate also conquers anxiety about the gods. The wise man by affirming his participation in universal reason transcends the realm of the gods. The courage to be transcends the polytheistic power of fate. The second assertion is that the soul of the wise man is similar to God. The God who is indicated here is the divine Logos in unity with whom the courage of wisdom conquers fate and transcends the gods. It is the "God above god." The third statement illustrates the difference of the idea of cosmic resignation from the idea of cosmic salvation in theistic terms. Seneca says that while God is *beyond* suffering the true Stoic is *above* it. Suffering, this implies, contradicts the nature of God. It is impossible for him to suffer, he is *beyond* it. The Stoic as a human being is able to suffer. But he need not let suffering conquer the center of his rational being. He can keep himself *above* it because it is a consequence of that which is not his essential being but is accidental in him. The distinction between "beyond" and "above" implies a value judgment. The wise man who courageously conquers desire, suffering, and anxiety "surpasses God himself." He is above the God who by his natural perfection and blessedness is beyond all this. On the basis of such a valuation the courage of wisdom and resignation could be replaced by the courage of faith in salvation, that is by faith in a God who paradoxically participates in human suffering. But Stoicism itself can never make this step.

Stoicism reaches its limits wherever the question is asked: How is the courage of wisdom possible? Although the Stoics emphasized that all human beings are equal in that they participate in the universal Logos, they could not deny the fact that wisdom is the possession of only an infinitely small elite. The masses of the people, they acknowledged, are "fools," in the bondage of desires and fears. While participating in the divine Logos with their essential or rational nature, most human beings are in a state of actual conflict with their own rationality and therefore unable to affirm their essential being courageously.

It was impossible for the Stoics to explain this situation

which they could not deny. And it was not only the pre-dominance of the "fools" among the masses that they could not explain. Something in the wise men themselves also faced them with a difficult problem. Seneca says that no courage is so great as that which is born of utter desper-ation. But, one must ask, has the Stoic as a Stoic reached the state of "utter desperation"? Can he reach it in the frame of his philosophy? Or is there something absent in his despair and consequently in his courage? The Stoic as a Stoic does not experience the despair of personal guilt. Epictetus quotes as an example Socrates' words in Xeno-phon's *Memorabilia* of Socrates: "I have maintained that which is under my control" and "I have never done any-thing that was wrong in my private or in my public life." And Epictetus himself asserts that he has learned not to care for anything that is outside the realm of his moral purpose. But more revealing than such statements is the general attitude of superiority and complacency which characterizes the Stoic *diatribai*, their moral orations and public accusations. The Stoic cannot say, as Hamlet does, that "conscience" makes cowards of us *all*. He does not see the universal fall from essential rationality to existen-tial foolishness as a matter of responsibility and as a prob-lem of guilt. The courage to be for him is the courage to affirm oneself in spite of fate and death, but it is not the courage to affirm oneself in spite of sin and guilt. It could not have been different: for the courage to face one's own guilt leads to the question of salvation instead of renuncia-tion.

COURAGE AND SELF-AFFIRMATION: SPINOZA

Stoicism retired into the background when faith in cosmic salvation replaced the courage of cosmic renunciation. But it returned when the medieval system which was dominated by the problem of salvation began to disintegrate. And it became decisive again for an intellectual elite which rejected the way of salvation without however replacing it with the Stoic way of renunciation. Because of the impact of Christianity on the Western world the revival of the ancient schools of thought at the beginning of the modern period was not only a revival but also a transformation. This is true of the revival of Platonism as well as of that of Skepticism and Stoicism; it is true of the renewal of the arts, of literature, of the theories of the state, and of the philosophy of religion. In all these cases the negativity of the late-ancient feeling toward life is transformed into the positiveness of the Christian ideas of creation and incarnation, even if these ideas are either ignored or denied. The spiritual substance of Renaissance humanism was Christian as the spiritual substance of ancient humanism was pagan, in spite of the criticism of the pagan religions by Greek humanism and of Christianity by modern humanism. The decisive difference between both types of humanism is the answer to the question whether being is essentially good or not. While the symbol of creation implies the classical Christian doctrine that "being as being is good" (*esse qua esse bonum est*) the doctrine of the "resisting matter" in Greek philosophy ex-

presses the pagan feeling that being is necessarily ambiguous insofar as it participates in both creative form and
inhibiting matter. This contrast in the basic ontological
conception has decisive consequences. While in later antiquity the various forms of metaphysical and religious
dualism are tied up with the ascetic ideal—the negation of
matter—the rebirth of antiquity in the modern period replaced asceticism by active shaping of the material realm.
And while in the ancient world the tragic feeling toward
existence dominated thought and life, especially the attitude toward history, the Renaissance started a movement
which was looking at the future and the creative and
new in it. Hope conquered the feeling of tragedy, and
belief in progress the resignation to circular repetition. A
third consequence of the basic ontological difference is
the contrast in the valuation of the individual on the part
of ancient and modern humanism. While the ancient
world valued the individual not as an individual but as
a representative of something universal, e.g. a virtue, the
rebirth of antiquity saw in the individual as an individual
a unique expression of the universe, incomparable, irreplaceable, and of infinite significance.

　It is obvious that these differences created decisive differences in the interpretation of courage. It is not the
contrast between renunciation and salvation to which I
am referring now. Modern humanism is still humanism,
rejecting the idea of salvation. But modern humanism
also rejects renunciation. It replaces it by a kind of self-
affirmation which transcends that of the Stoics because

it includes the material, historical, and individual existence. Nevertheless, there are so many points in which
this modern humanism is identical with ancient Stoicism
that it may be called Neo-Stoicism. Spinoza is its representative. In him as in nobody else the ontology of courage is elaborated. In calling his main ontological work
Ethics he indicated in the title itself his intention to show
the ontological foundation of man's ethical existence,
including man's courage to be. But for Spinoza—as for
the Stoics—the courage to be is not one thing beside
others. It is an expression of the essential act of everything
that participates in being, namely self-affirmation. The
doctrine of self-affirmation is a central element in Spinoza's thought. Its decisive character is manifest in a proposition like this: "The endeavour, wherewith everything
endeavours to persist in its own being, is nothing else
but the actual essence of the thing in question" (*Ethics*
iii. prop. 7). The * Latin word for endeavor is *conatus*,
the striving toward something. This striving is not a contingent aspect of a thing, nor is it an element in its being
along with other elements; it is its *essentia actualis*. The
conatus makes a thing what it is, so that if it disappears the
thing itself disappears (*Ethics* ii, Def. 2). Striving toward
self-preservation or toward self-affirmation makes a thing
be what it is. Spinoza calls this striving which is the essence
of a thing also its power, and he says of the mind that
it affirms or posits (*affirmat sive ponit*) its own power

* The Chief Works of Benedict de Spinoza, trans. R. H. M.
Elwes (London, Bell and Sons, 1919).

of action (*ipsius agendi potentiam*) (iii. prop. 54). So we have the identification of actual essence, power of being, and self-affirmation. And more identifications follow. The power of being is identified with virtue, and virtue consequently, with essential nature. Virtue is the power of acting exclusively according to one's true nature. And the degree of virtue is the degree to which somebody is striving for and able to affirm his own being. It is impossible to conceive of any virtue as prior to the striving to preserve one's own being (iv. prop. 22). Self-affirmation is, so to speak, virtue altogether. But self-affirmation is affirmation of one's essential being, and the knowledge of one's essential being is mediated through reason, the power of the soul to have adequate ideas. Therefore to act unconditionally out of virtue is the same as to act under the guidance of reason, to affirm one's essential being or true nature (iv. prop. 24).

On this basis the relation of courage and self-affirmation is explained. Spinoza (iii. prop. 59) uses two terms, *fortitudo* and *animositas*. Fortitudo (as in the Scholastic terminology) is the strength of the soul, its power to be what it essentially is. Animositas, derived from *anima*, soul, is courage in the sense of a total act of the person. Its definition is this: "By courage I mean the desire [*cupiditas*] whereby every man strives to preserve his own being in accordance solely with the dictates of reason" (iii. prop. 59). This definition would lead to another identification, of courage with virtue in general. But Spinoza distinguishes between *animositas* and *generositas*, the desire to join other people in friendship and support. This duality of an all-embracing and a limited concept of courage corresponds with the whole development of the idea of courage to which we have referred. In a systematic philosophy of the strictness and consistency of Spinoza's this is a remarkable fact and shows the two cognitive motives which always determine the doctrine of courage: the universally ontological and the specifically moral. This has a very significant consequence for one of the most difficult ethical problems, the relation of self-affirmation and love toward others. For Spinoza the latter is an implication of the former. Since virtue and the power of self-affirmation are identical, and since "generosity" is the act of going out toward others in a benevolent affect, no conflict between self-affirmation and love can be thought of. This of course presupposes that self-affirmation is not only distinguished from but precisely the opposite of "selfishness" in the sense of a negative moral quality. Self-affirmation is the ontological opposite of the "reduction of being" by such affects as contradict one's essential nature. Erich Fromm has fully expressed the idea that the right self-love and the right love of others are interdependent, and that selfishness and the abuse of others are equally interdependent. Spinoza's doctrine of self-affirmation include both the right self-love (although he does not use the term self-love, which I myself hesitate to use) and the right love of others.

Self-affirmation, according to Spinoza, is participation in the divine self-affirmation. "The power whereby each particular thing, and consequently man, preserves his being is the power of God" (iv. prop. 4). The participation of the soul in the divine power is described in terms of both knowledge and love. If the soul recognizes itself "sub aeternitatis specie" (v. prop. 30), it recognizes its being in God. And this knowledge of God and of its being in God is the cause of perfect beatitude and consequently of a perfect love toward the cause of this beatitude. This love is spiritual (*intellectualis*) because it is eternal and therefore an affect, not subject to the passions which are connected with bodily existence (v. prop. 34). It is the participation in the infinite spiritual love with which God contemplates and loves himself, and by loving himself also loves what belongs to him, human beings. These statements answer two questions about the nature of courage which had remained unanswered. They explain why self-affirmation is the essential nature of every being and as such its highest good. Perfect self-affirmation is not an isolated act which originates in the individual being but is participation in the universal or divine act of self-affirmation, which is the originating power in every individual act. In this idea the ontology of courage has reached its fundamental expression. And a second question is answered, that of the power which makes the conquest of desire and anxiety possible. The Stoics had no answer to that. Spinoza, out of his Jewish mysticism, answers with the idea of participation. He knows that an affect can be conquered only by another affect, and that the only affect which can overcome the affects of passion is the affect of the mind, the spiritual or intellectual love of the soul for its own eternal ground. This affect is an expression of the participation of the soul in the divine self-love. The courage to be is possible because it is participation in the self-affirmation of being-itself.

One question, however, remains unanswered, by Spinoza as well as by the Stoics. It is the question formulated by Spinoza himself at the end of his *Ethics*. Why, he asks, is it that the way of salvation (*salus*) which he has shown is being neglected by almost everyone? Because it is difficult and therefore rare, like everything sublime, he answers in the melancholy last sentence of his book. This was also the answer of the Stoics, but it is an answer not of salvation but of resignation.

COURAGE AND LIFE: NIETZSCHE

Spinoza's concept of self-preservation as well as our interpretative concept "self-affirmation," if taken ontologically, posit a serious question. What does self-affirmation mean if there is no self, e.g. in the inorganic realm or in the infinite substance, in being-itself? Is it not an argument against the ontological character of courage that it is impossible to attribute courage to large sections of reality and to the essence of all reality? Is courage not a human quality which can be attributed even to higher animals only by analogy but not properly? Does this not decide for the moral against the ontological understanding of courage? In stating this argument one is reminded of similar arguments against most metaphysical concepts in the history of human thought. Concepts like world soul, microcosmos, instinct, the will to power, and so on have been accused of introducing subjectivity into the objective realm of things. But these accusations are mistaken. They miss the meaning of ontological concepts. It is not the function of these concepts to describe the ontological nature of reality in terms of the subjective or the objective side of our ordinary experience. It is the function of an ontological concept to use some realm of experience to point to characteristics of being-itself which lie above the split between subjectivity and objectivity and which therefore cannot be expressed literally in terms taken from the subjective or the objective side. Ontology speaks analogously. Being as being transcends objectivity as well as subjectivity. But in order to approach it cognitively one must use both. And one can do so because both are rooted in that which transcends them, in being-itself. It is the light of this consideration that the ontological concepts referred to must be interpreted. They must be understood not literally but analogously. This does not mean that they have been produced arbitrarily and can easily be replaced by other concepts. Their choice is a matter of experience and thought, and subject to criteria which determine the adequacy or inadequacy of each of them. This is true also of concepts like self-preservation or self-affirmation, if taken in an ontological sense. It is true of every chapter of an ontology of courage.

Both self-preservation and self-affirmation logically imply the overcoming of something which, at least potentially, threatens or denies the self. There is no explanation of this "something" in either Stoicism or Neo-Stoicism, though both presuppose it. In the case of Spinoza it even seems impossible to account for such a negative element in the frame of his system. If everything follows by necessity from the nature of the eternal substance, no being would have the power to threaten the self-preservation of another being. Everything would be as it is and self-affirmation would be an exaggerated word for the simple identity of a thing with itself. But this certainly is not Spinoza's opinion. He speaks of a real threat and even of his experience that most people succumb to this threat. He speaks of *conatus*, the striving for, and of *potentia*, the power of self-realization. These words, though they cannot be taken literally cannot be dismissed as meaningless either. They must be taken analogously. From Plato and Aristotle on, the concept of power plays an important role in ontological thought. Terms like *dynamis*, *potentia* (Leibnitz) as characterizations of the true nature of being prepare the way for Nietzsche's "will to power." So does the term "will" used for ultimate reality from Augustine and Duns Scotus on to Boehme, Schelling, and Schopenhauer. Nietzsche's will to power unites both terms and must be understood in the light of their ontological meaning. One could say paradoxically that Nietzsche's will to power is neither will nor power, that is, is neither will in the psychological sense nor power in the sociological sense. It designates the self-affirmation of life as life, including self-preservation and growth. Therefore the will does not strive for something it does not have, for some object outside itself, but wills itself in the double sense of preserving and transcending itself. This is its power, and also its power over itself. Will to power is the self-affirmation of the will as ultimate reality.

Nietzsche is the most impressive and effective representative of what could be called a "philosophy of life." Life in this term is the process in which the power of being actualizes itself. But in actualizing itself it overcomes that in life which, although belonging to life, negates life. One could call it the will which contradicts the will to power. In his *Zarathustra*, in the chapter called "The Preachers of Death" (Pt. I, chap. 9), Nietzsche points to the different ways in which life is tempted to accept its own negation: "They meet an invalid, or an old man, or a corpse— and immediately they say: 'Life is refuted!' But they only are refuted, and their eye, which seeth only one aspect of existence." * Life has many aspects, it is ambiguous. Nietzsche has described its ambiguity most typically in the last fragment of the collection of fragments which is called the *Will to Power*. Courage is the power of life to affirm itself in spite of this ambiguity, while the negation of life because of its negativity is an expression of cowardice. On this basis Nietzsche develops a prophecy and philosophy of courage in opposition to

* The Complete Works of Friedrich Nietzsche, ed. Oscar Levy (London, T. N. Foulis, 1911), Vol. *11*, trans. Thomas Common.

the mediocrity and decadence of life in the period whose coming he saw.

Like the earlier philosophers Nietzsche in *Zarathustra* considered the "warrior" (whom he distinguishes from the mere soldier) an outstanding example of courage. " 'What is good?' ye ask. To be brave is good" (I, 10), not to be interested in long life, not to want to be spared, and all this just because of the love for life. The death of the warrior and of the mature man shall not be a reproach to the earth (I, 21). Self-affirmation is the affirmation of life and of the death which belongs to life.

Virtue for Nietzsche as for Spinoza is self-affirmation. In the chapter on "The Virtuous" Nietzsche writes: "It is your dearest Self, your virtue. The ring's thirst is in you: to reach itself again struggleth every ring, and turn-eth itself" (II, 27). This analogy describes better than any definition the meaning of self-affirmation in the philosophy of life: The Self has itself, but at the same time it tries to reach itself. Here Spinoza's *conatus* becomes dynamic, as, generally speaking, one could say that Nietzsche is a revival of Spinoza in dynamic terms: "Life" in Nietzsche replaces "substance" in Spinoza. And this is true not only of Nietzsche but of most of the philosophers of life. The truth of virtue is that the Self is in it "and not an outward thing." "That *your* very Self be in your action, as the mother is in the child: let that be *your* formula of virtue!" (II, 27.) Insofar as courage is the affirmation of one's self it is virtue altogether. The self whose self-affirmation is virtue and courage is the self which surpasses itself: "And this secret spake Life herself unto me. 'Behold,' said she, 'I am that *which must ever surpass itself*'" (II, 34). By italicizing the last words Nietzsche indicates that he wants to give a definition of the essential nature of life. ". . . There doth Life sacrifice itself—for power!" he continues, and shows in these words that for him self-affirmation includes self-negation, not for the sake of negation but for the sake of the greatest possible affirmation, for what he calls "power." Life creates and life loves what it has created—but soon it must turn against it: "so willeth my [Life's] will." Therefore it is wrong to speak of "will to existence" or even of "will to life"; one must speak of "will to power," i.e. to more life.

Life, willing to surpass itself, is the good life, and the good life is the courageous life. It is the life of the "powerful soul" and the "triumphant body" whose self-enjoyment is virtue. Such a soul banishes "everything cowardly; it says: bad—that is cowardly" (III, 54). But in order to reach such a nobility it is necessary to obey and to command and to obey while commanding. This obedience which is included in commanding is the opposite of submissiveness. The latter is the cowardice which does not dare to risk itself. The submissive self is the opposite of the self-affirming self, even if it is submissive to a God. It wants to escape the pain of hurting and being hurt. The obedient self, on the contrary, is the self which commands itself and "risketh itself thereby" (II, 34). In commanding itself it becomes its own judge and its own victim. It commands itself according to the law of life, the law of self-transcendence. The will which commands itself is the creative will. It makes a whole out of fragments and riddles of life. It does not look back, it stands beyond a bad conscience, it rejects the "spirit of revenge" which is the innermost nature of self-accusation and of the consciousness of guilt, it transcends reconciliation, for it is the will to power (II, 42). In doing all this the courageous self is united with life itself and its secret (II, 34).

We may conclude our discussion of Nietzsche's ontology of courage with the following quotation: "Have ye courage, O my brethren? . . . *Not* the courage before witnesses, but anchorite and eagle courage, which not even a God any longer beholdeth? . . . He hath heart who knoweth fear but *vanquisheth* it; who seeth the abyss, but with *pride*. He who seeth the abyss but with eagle's eyes,—he who with eagle's talons *graspeth* the abyss: he hath courage" (IV, 73, sec. 4).

These words reveal the other side of Nietzsche, that in him which makes him an Existentialist, the courage to look into the abyss of nonbeing in the complete loneliness of him who accepts the message that "God is dead." About this side we shall have more to say in the following chapters. At this point we must close our historical survey, which was not meant to be a history of the idea of courage. It had a double purpose. It was supposed to show that in the history of Western thought from Plato's *Laches* to Nietzsche's *Zarathustra* the ontological problem of courage has attracted creative philosophy, partly because the moral character of courage remains incomprehensible without its ontological character, partly because the experience of courage proved to be an outstanding key for the ontological approach to reality. And further, the historical survey is meant to present conceptual material for the systematic treatment of the problem of courage, above all the concept of ontological self-affirmation in its basic character and its different interpretations.

AN ONTOLOGY OF ANXIETY

THE MEANING OF NONBEING

Courage is self-affirmation "in-spite-of," that is in spite of that which tends to prevent the self from affirming itself. Differing from the Stoic–Neo-Stoic doctrines of courage, the "philosophies of life" have seriously and affirmatively dealt with that against which courage stands. For if being is interpreted in terms of life or process or becoming, nonbeing is ontologically as basic as being. The acknowledgment of this fact does not imply a decision about the priority of being over nonbeing, but it requires a consideration of nonbeing in the very foundation of ontology. Speaking of courage as a key to the interpretation of being-itself, one could say that this key, when it opens the door to being, finds, at the same time, being and the negation of being and their unity.

Nonbeing is one of the most difficult and most discussed concepts. Parmenides tried to remove it as a concept. But in order to do so he had to sacrifice life. Democritus re-established it and identified it with empty space, in order to make movement thinkable. Plato used the concept of nonbeing because without it the contrast of existence with the pure essences is beyond understanding. It is implied in Aristotle's distinction between matter and form. It gave Plotinus the means of describing the loss of self of the human soul, and it gave Augustine the means for an ontological interpretation of human sin. For Pseudo-Dionysius the Areopagite nonbeing became the principle of his mystical doctrine of God. Jacob Boehme, the Protestant mystic and philosopher of life, made the classical statement that all things are rooted in a Yes and a No. In Leibnitz' doctrine of finitude and evil as well as in Kant's analysis of the finitude of categorical forms nonbeing is implied. Hegel's dialectic makes negation the dynamic power in nature and history; and the philosophers of life, since Schelling and Schopenhauer, use "will" as the basic ontological category because it has the power of negating itself without losing itself. The concepts of process and becoming in philosophers like Bergson and Whitehead imply nonbeing as well as being. Recent Existentialists, especially Heidegger and Sartre, have put nonbeing (*Das Nichts, le néant*) in the center of their ontological thought; and Berdyaev, a follower of both Dionysius and Boehme, has developed an ontology of nonbeing which accounts for the "me-ontic" freedom in God and man. These philosophical ways of using the concept of nonbeing can be viewed against the background of the religious experience of the transitoriness of everything created and the power of the "demonic" in the human soul and history. In biblical religion these negativities have a decisive place in spite of the doctrine of creation. And the demonic, anti-divine principle, which never-theless participates in the power of the divine, appears in the dramatic centers of the biblical story.

In view of this situation it is of little significance that some logicians deny that nonbeing has conceptual char-acter and try to remove it from the philosophical scene except in the form of negative judgments. For the ques-tion is: What does the fact of negative judgments tell about the character of being? What is the ontological condition of negative judgments? How is the realm con-stituted in which negative judgments are possible? Cer-tainly nonbeing is not a concept like others. It is the nega-tion of every concept; but as such it is an inescapable content of thought and, as the history of thought has shown, the most important one after being-itself.

If one is asked how nonbeing is related to being-itself, one can only answer metaphorically: being "embraces" itself and nonbeing. Being has nonbeing "within" itself as that which is eternally present and eternally overcome in the process of the divine life. The ground of everything that is is not a dead identity without movement and be-coming; it is living creativity. Creatively it affirms itself, eternally conquering its own nonbeing. As such it is the pattern of the self-affirmation of every finite being and the source of the courage to be.

Courage is usually described as the power of the mind to overcome fear. The meaning of fear seemed too obvious to deserve inquiry. But in the last decades depth psychol-ogy in cooperation with Existentialist philosophy has led to a sharp distinction between fear and anxiety and to more precise definitions of each of these concepts. Sociological analyses of the present period have pointed to the importance of anxiety as a group phenomenon. Literature and art have made anxiety a main theme of their creations, in content as well as in style. The effect of this has been the awakening of at least the educated groups to an awareness of their own anxiety, and a permeation of the public consciousness by ideas and symbols of anxiety. Today it has become almost a truism to call our time an "age of anxiety." This holds equally for America and Europe.

Nevertheless it is necessary for an ontology of courage to include an ontology of anxiety, for they are interdependent. And it is conceivable that in the light of an ontology of courage some fundamental aspects of anxiety may become visible. The first assertion about the nature of anxiety is this: anxiety is the state in which a being is aware of its possible nonbeing. The same statement, in a shorter form, would read: anxiety is the existential awareness of nonbeing. "Existential" in this sentence means that it is not the abstract knowledge of nonbeing which produces anxiety but the awareness that nonbeing is a part of one's own being. It is not the realization of universal transitoriness, not even the experience of the death of others, but the impression of these events on the always latent awareness of our own having to die that produces anxiety. Anxiety is finitude, experienced as one's own finitude. This is the natural anxiety of man as man, and in some way of all living beings. It is the anxiety of nonbeing, the awareness of one's finitude as finitude.

THE INTERDEPENDENCE
OF FEAR AND ANXIETY

Anxiety and fear have the same ontological root but they are not the same in actuality. This is common knowledge, but it has been emphasized and overemphasized to such a degree that a reaction against it may occur and wipe out not only the exaggerations but also the truth of the distinction. Fear, as opposed to anxiety has a definite object (as most authors agree), which can be faced, analyzed, attacked, endured. One can act upon it, and in acting upon it participate in it—even if in the form of struggle. In this way one can take it into one's self-affirmation. Courage can meet every object of fear, because it is an object and makes participation possible. Courage can take the fear produced by a definite object into itself, because this object, however frightful it may be, has a side with which it participates in us and we in it. One could say that as long as there is an *object* of fear love in the sense of participation can conquer fear.

But this is not so with anxiety, because anxiety has no object, or rather, in a paradoxical phrase, its object is the negation of every object. Therefore participation, struggle, and love with respect to it are impossible. He who is in anxiety is, insofar as it is mere anxiety, delivered to it without help. Helplessness in the state of anxiety can be observed in animals and humans alike. It expresses itself in loss of direction, inadequate reactions, lack of "intentionality" (the being related to meaningful contents of knowledge or will). The reason for this sometimes striking behavior is the lack of an object on which the subject (in the state of anxiety) can concentrate. The only object is the threat itself, but not the source of the threat, because the source of the threat is "nothingness."

One might ask whether this threatening "nothing" is not the unknown, the indefinite possibility of an actual threat? Does not anxiety cease in the moment in which a known object of fear appears? Anxiety then would be fear of the unknown. But this is an insufficient explanation of anxiety. For there are innumerable realms of the unknown, different for each subject, and faced without any anxiety. It is the unknown of a special type which is met with anxiety. It is the unknown which by its very nature cannot be known, because it is nonbeing.

Fear and anxiety are distinguished but not separated. They are immanent within each other: The sting of fear is anxiety, and anxiety strives toward fear. Fear is being afraid of something, a pain, the rejection by a person or a group, the loss of something or somebody, the moment of dying. But in the anticipation of the threat originating in these things, it is not the negativity itself which they will bring upon the subject that is frightening but the anxiety about the possible implications of this negativity. The outstanding example—and more than an example— is the fear of dying. Insofar as it is *fear* its object is the anticipated event of being killed by sickness or an acci-

dent and thereby suffering agony and the loss of everything. Insofar as it is *anxiety* its object is the absolutely
unknown "after death," the nonbeing which remains nonbeing even if it is filled with images of our present experience. The dreams in Hamlet's soliloquy, "to be or not to
be," which we may have after death and which make
cowards of us all are frightful not because of their manifest content but because of their power to symbolize the
threat of nothingness, in religious terms of "eternal death."
The symbols of hell created by Dante produce anxiety not
because of their objective imagery but because they express the "nothingness" whose power is experienced in the
anxiety of guilt. Each of the situations described in the
Inferno could be met by courage on the basis of participation and love. But of course the meaning is that this is
impossible; in other words they are not real situations but
symbols of the objectless, of nonbeing.

The fear of death determines the element of anxiety in
every fear. Anxiety, if not modified by the fear of an
object, anxiety in its nakedness, is always the anxiety of
ultimate nonbeing. Immediately seen, anxiety is the pain-
ful feeling of not being able to deal with the threat of a
special situation. But a more exact analysis shows that in
the anxiety about any special situation anxiety about the
human situation as such is implied. It is the anxiety of not
being able to preserve one's own being which underlies
every fear and is the frightening element in it. In the moment, therefore, in which "naked anxiety" lays hold of

the mind, the previous objects of fear cease to be definite objects. They appear as what they always were in part, symptoms of man's basic anxiety. As such they are beyond the reach of even the most courageous attack upon them.

This situation drives the anxious subject to establish objects of fear. Anxiety strives to become fear, because fear can be met by courage. It is impossible for a finite being to stand naked anxiety for more than a flash of time. People who have experienced these moments, as for instance some mystics in their visions of the "night of the soul," or Luther under the despair of the demonic assaults, or Nietzsche-Zarathustra in the experience of the "great disgust," have told of the unimaginable horror of it. This horror is ordinarily avoided by the transformation of anxiety into fear of something, no matter what. The human mind is not only, as Calvin has said, a permanent factory of idols, it is also a permanent factory of fears— the first in order to escape God, the second in order to escape anxiety; and there is a relation between the two. For facing the God who is really God means facing also the absolute threat of nonbeing. The "naked absolute" (to use a phrase of Luther's) produces "naked anxiety"; for it is the extinction of every finite self-affirmation, and not a possible object of fear and courage. (See Chapters 5 and 6.) But ultimately the attempts to transform anxiety into fear are vain. The basic anxiety, the anxiety of a finite being about the threat of nonbeing, cannot be eliminated. It belongs to existence itself.

Types of Anxiety

THE THREE TYPES OF ANXIETY
AND THE NATURE OF MAN

Nonbeing is dependent on the being it negates. "Dependent" means two things. It points first of all to the ontological priority of being over nonbeing. The term nonbeing itself indicates this, and it is logically necessary. There could be no negation if there were no preceding affirmation to be negated. Certainly one can describe being in terms of non-nonbeing; and one can justify such a description by pointing to the astonishing prerational fact that there is something and not nothing. One could say that "being is the negation of the primordial night of nothingness." But in doing so one must realize that such an aboriginal nothing would be neither nothing nor something, that it becomes nothing only in contrast to something; in other words, that the ontological status of nonbeing as nonbeing is dependent on being. Secondly, nonbeing is dependent on the special qualities of being. In itself nonbeing has no quality and no difference of qualities. But it gets them in relation to being. The character of the negation of being is determined by that in being which is negated. This makes it possible to speak of qualities of nonbeing and, consequently, of types of anxiety.

Up to now we have used the term nonbeing without differentiation, while in the discussion of courage several forms of self-affirmation were mentioned. They correspond to different forms of anxiety and are understandable only in correlation with them. I suggest that we distinguish three types of anxiety according to the three directions in which nonbeing threatens being. Nonbeing threatens man's ontic self-affirmation, relatively in terms of fate, absolutely in terms of death. It threatens man's spiritual self-affirmation, relatively in terms of emptiness, absolutely in terms of meaninglessness. It threatens man's moral self-affirmation, relatively in terms of guilt, absolutely in terms of condemnation. The awareness of this threefold threat is anxiety appearing in three forms, that of fate and death (briefly, the anxiety of death), that of emptiness and loss of meaning (briefly, the anxiety of meaninglessness), that of guilt and condemnation (briefly, the anxiety of condemnation). In all three forms anxiety is existential in the sense that it belongs to existence as such and not to an abnormal state of mind as in neurotic (and psychotic) anxiety. The nature of neurotic anxiety and its relation to existential anxiety will be discussed in another chapter. We shall deal now with the three forms of existential anxiety, first with their reality in the life of the individual, then with their social manifestations in special periods of Western history. However, it must be stated that the difference of types does not mean mutual exclusion. In the first chapter we have seen for instance that the courage to be as it appears in the ancient Stoics conquers not only the fear of death but also the threat of meaninglessness. In Nietzsche we find that in spite of the predominance of the threat of meaninglessness, the

anxiety of death and condemnation is passionately challenged. In all representatives of classical Christianity death
and sin are seen as the allied adversaries against which the
courage of faith has to fight. The three forms of anxiety
(and of courage) are immanent in each other but normally
under the dominance of one of them.

THE ANXIETY OF FATE AND DEATH

Fate and death are the way in which our ontic self-
affirmation is threatened by nonbeing. "Ontic," from the
Greek *on*, "being," means here the basic self-affirmation
of a being in its simple existence. (Onto-logical designates the philosophical analysis of the nature of being.)
The anxiety of fate and death is most basic, most universal,
and inescapable. All attempts to argue it away are futile.
Even if the so-called arguments for the "immortality of
the soul" had argumentative power (which they do not
have) they would not convince existentially. For existentially everybody is aware of the complete loss of self
which biological extinction implies. The unsophisticated
mind knows instinctively what sophisticated ontology
formulates: that reality has the basic structure of self-
world correlation and that with the disappearance of the
one side the world, the other side, the self, also disappears,
and what remains is their common ground but not their
structural correlation. It has been observed that the anxiety of death increases with the increase of individualization and that people in collectivistic cultures are less open
to this type of anxiety. The observation is correct yet the

explanation that there is no basic anxiety about death in collectivist cultures is wrong. The reason for the difference from more individualized civilizations is that the special type of courage which characterizes collectivism (see pp. 92 f.), as long as it is unshaken, allays the anxiety of death. But the very fact that courage has to be created through many internal and external (psychological and ritual) activities and symbols shows that basic anxiety has to be overcome even in collectivism. Without its at least potential presence neither war nor the criminal law in these societies would be understandable. If there were no fear of death, the threat of the law or of a superior enemy would be without effect—which it obviously is not. Man as man in every civilization is anxiously aware of the threat of nonbeing and needs the courage to affirm himself in spite of it.

The anxiety of death is the permanent horizon within which the anxiety of fate is at work. For the threat against man's ontic self-affirmation is not only the absolute threat of death but also the relative threat of fate. Certainly the anxiety of death overshadows all concrete anxieties and gives them their ultimate seriousness. They have, however, a certain independence and, ordinarily, a more immediate impact than the anxiety of death. The term "fate" for this whole group of anxieties stresses one element which is common to all of them: their contingent character, their unpredictability, the impossibility of showing their meaning and purpose. One can describe this in terms of the categorical structure of our experience. One

can show the contingency of our temporal being, the fact
that we exist in this and no other period of time, beginning
in a contingent moment, ending in a contingent moment,
filled with experiences which are contingent themselves
with respect to quality and quantity. One can show the
contingency of our spatial being (our finding ourselves
in this and no other place, and the strangeness of this
place in spite of its familiarity); the contingent character
of ourselves and the place from which we look at our
world; and the contingent character of the reality at
which we look, that is, our world. Both could be different: this is their contingency and this produces the
anxiety about our spatial existence. One can show the
contingency of the causal interdependence of which one
is a part, both with respect to the past and to the present,
the vicissitudes coming from our world and the hidden
forces in the depths of our own self. Contingent does
not mean causally undetermined but it means that the de-
termining causes of our existence have no ultimate necessity. They are given, and they cannot be logically derived.
Contingently we are put into the whole web of causal
relations. Contingently we are determined by them in
every moment and thrown out by them in the last moment.

   Fate is the rule of contingency, and the anxiety about
fate is based on the finite being's awareness of being contingent in every respect, of having no ultimate necessity.
Fate is usually identified with necessity in the sense of an
inescapable causal determination. Yet it is not causal

necessity that makes fate a matter of anxiety but the lack of ultimate necessity, the irrationality, the impenetrable darkness of fate.

The threat of nonbeing to man's ontic self-affirmation is absolute in the threat of death, relative in the threat of fate. But the relative threat is a threat only because in its background stands the absolute threat. Fate would not produce inescapable anxiety without death behind it. And death stands behind fate and its contingencies not only in the last moment when one is thrown out of existence but in every moment within existence. Nonbeing is omnipresent and produces anxiety even where an immediate threat of death is absent. It stands behind the experience that we are driven, together with everything else, from the past toward the future without a moment of time which does not vanish immediately. It stands behind the insecurity and homelessness of our social and individual existence. It stands behind the attacks on our power of being in body and soul by weakness, disease, and accidents. In all these forms fate actualizes itself, and through them the anxiety of nonbeing takes hold of us. We try to transform the anxiety into fear and to meet courageously the objects in which the threat is embodied. We succeed partly, but somehow we are aware of the fact that it is not these objects with which we struggle that produce the anxiety but the human situation as such. Out of this the question arises: Is there a courage to be, a courage to affirm oneself in spite of the threat against man's ontic self-affirmation?

THE ANXIETY OF EMPTINESS
AND MEANINGLESSNESS

Nonbeing threatens man as a whole, and therefore threatens his spiritual as well as his ontic self-affirmation. Spiritual self-affirmation occurs in every moment in which man lives creatively in the various spheres of meaning. Creative, in this context, has the sense not of original creativity as performed by the genius but of living spontaneously, in action and reaction, with the contents of one's cultural life. In order to be spiritually creative one need not be what is called a creative artist or scientist or statesman, but one must be able to participate meaningfully in their original creations. Such a participation is creative insofar as it changes that in which one participates, even if in very small ways. The creative transformation of a language by the interdependence of the creative poet or writer and the many who are influenced by him directly or indirectly and react spontaneously to him is an outstanding example. Everyone who lives creatively in meanings affirms himself as a participant in these meanings. He affirms himself as receiving and transforming reality creatively. He loves himself as participating in the spiritual life and as loving its contents. He loves them because they are his own fulfillment and because they are actualized through him. The scientist loves both the truth he discovers and himself insofar as he discovers it. He is held by the content of his discovery. This is what one can call "spiritual self-affirmation." And if he has not discovered but only participates in the discovery, it is equally spiritual self-affirmation.

Such an experience presupposes that the spiritual life is taken seriously, that it is a matter of ultimate concern. And this again presupposes that in it and through it ultimate reality becomes manifest. A spiritual life in which this is not experienced is threatened by nonbeing in the two forms in which it attacks spiritual self-affirmation: emptiness and meaninglessness.

We use the term meaninglessness for the absolute threat of nonbeing to spiritual self-affirmation, and the term emptiness for the relative threat to it. They are no more identical than are the threat of death and fate. But in the background of emptiness lies meaninglessness as death lies in the background of the vicissitudes of fate.

The anxiety of meaninglessness is anxiety about the loss of an ultimate concern, of a meaning which gives meaning to all meanings. This anxiety is aroused by the loss of a spiritual center, of an answer, however symbolic and indirect, to the question of the meaning of existence.

The anxiety of emptiness is aroused by the threat of nonbeing to the special contents of the spiritual life. A belief breaks down through external events or inner processes: one is cut off from creative participation in a sphere of culture, one feels frustrated about something which one had passionately affirmed, one is driven from devotion to one object to devotion to another and again on to another, because the meaning of each of them vanishes and the creative eros is transformed into indifference or aversion. Everything is tried and nothing satisfies. The contents of the tradition, however excellent, however praised, however loved once, lose their power to give content *today*. And present culture is even less able to provide the content. Anxiously one turns away from all concrete contents and looks for an ultimate meaning, only to discover that it was precisely the loss of a spiritual center which took away the meaning from the special contents of the spiritual life. But a spiritual center cannot be produced intentionally, and the attempt to produce it only produces deeper anxiety. The anxiety of emptiness drives us to the abyss of meaninglessness.

Emptiness and loss of meaning are expressions of the threat of nonbeing to the spiritual life. This threat is implied in man's finitude and actualized by man's estrangement. It can be described in terms of doubt, its creative and its destructive function in man's spiritual life. Man is able to ask because he is separated *from*, while participating *in*, what he is asking about. In every question an element of doubt, the awareness of not having, is implied. In systematic questioning systematic doubt is effective; e.g. of the Cartesian type. This element of doubt is a condition of all spiritual life. The threat to spiritual life is not doubt as an element but the total doubt. If the awareness of not having has swallowed the awareness of having, doubt has ceased to be methodological asking and has become existential despair. On the way to this situation the spiritual life tries to maintain itself as long as possible by clinging to affirmations which are not yet undercut, be they traditions, autonomous convictions, or emotional preferences. And if it is impossible to remove the doubt, one courageously accepts it without surrendering one's convictions. One takes the risk of going astray and the anxiety of this risk upon oneself. In this way one avoids the extreme situation—till it becomes unavoidable and the despair of truth becomes complete.

Then man tries another way out: Doubt is based on man's separation from the whole of reality, on his lack of universal participation, on the isolation of his individual self. So he tries to break out of this situation, to identify himself with something transindividual, to surrender his separation and self-relatedness. He flees from his freedom of asking and answering for himself to a situation in which no further questions can be asked and the answers to previous questions are imposed on him authoritatively. In order to avoid the risk of asking and doubting he surrenders the right to ask and to doubt. He surrenders himself in order to save his spiritual life. He "escapes from his freedom" (Fromm) in order to escape the anxiety of meaninglessness. Now he is no longer lonely, not in existential doubt, not in despair. He "participates" and affirms by participation the contents of his spiritual life. Meaning is saved, but the self is sacrificed. And since the conquest of doubt was a matter of sacrifice, the sacrifice of the freedom of the self, it leaves a mark on the regained certitude: a fanatical self-assertiveness. Fanaticism is the correlate to spiritual self-surrender: it shows the anxiety which it was supposed to conquer, by attacking with disproportionate violence those who disagree and who demonstrate by their disagreement elements in the spiritual life of the fanatic which he must suppress in himself. Because he must suppress them in himself he must suppress them in others. His anxiety forces him to persecute dissenters. The weakness of the fanatic is that those whom he fights have a secret hold upon him; and to this weakness he and his group finally succumb.

It is not always personal doubt that undermines and empties a system of ideas and values. It can be the fact that they are no longer understood in their original power of expressing the human situation and of answering existential human questions. (This is largely the case with the doctrinal symbols of Christianity.) Or they lose their meaning because the actual conditions of the present period are so different from those in which the spiritual contents were created that new creations are needed. (This was largely the case with artistic expression before the industrial revolution.) In such circumstances a slow process of waste of the spiritual contents occurs, unnoticeable in the beginning, realized with a shock as it progresses, producing the anxiety of meaninglessness at its end.

Ontic and spiritual self-affirmation must be distinguished but they cannot be separated. Man's being includes his relation to meanings. He is human only by understanding and shaping reality, both his world and himself, according to meanings and values. His being is spiritual even in the most primitive expressions of the most primitive human being. In the "first" meaningful sentence all the richness of man's spiritual life is potentially present. Therefore the threat to his spiritual being is a threat to his whole being. The most revealing expression of this fact is the desire to throw away one's ontic existence rather than stand the despair of emptiness and meaninglessness. The death instinct is not an ontic but a spiritual phenomenon. Freud identified this reaction to the meaninglessness of the never-ceasing and never-satisfied libido with man's essential nature. But it is only an expression of his existential self-estrangement and of the disintegration of his spiritual life into meaninglessness. If, on the other hand, the ontic self-affirmation is weakened by nonbeing, spiritual indifference and emptiness can be the consequence, producing a circle of ontic and spiritual negativity. Nonbeing threatens from both sides, the ontic and the spiritual; if it threatens the one side it also threatens the other.

THE ANXIETY OF GUILT AND CONDEMNATION

Nonbeing threatens from a third side; it threatens man's moral self-affirmation. Man's being, ontic as well as spiritual, is not only given to him but also demanded of him. He is responsible for it; literally, he is required to answer, if he is asked, what he has made of himself. He who asks him is his judge, namely he himself, who, at the same time, stands against him. This situation produces the anxiety which, in relative terms, is the anxiety of guilt; in

absolute terms, the anxiety of self-rejection or condemnation. Man is essentially "finite freedom"; freedom not in
the sense of indeterminacy but in the sense of being able
to determine himself through decisions in the center of
his being. Man, as finite freedom, is free within the contingencies of his finitude. But within these limits he is
asked to make of himself what he is supposed to become,
to fulfill his destiny. In every act of moral self-affirmation
man contributes to the fulfillment of his destiny, to the
actualization of what he potentially is. It is the task of
ethics to describe the nature of this fulfillment, in philosophical or theological terms. But however the norm is
formulated man has the power of acting against it, of
contradicting his essential being, of losing his destiny.
And under the conditions of man's estrangement from
himself this is an actuality. Even in what he considers his
best deed nonbeing is present and prevents it from being
perfect. A profound ambiguity between good and evil
permeates everything he does, because it permeates his
personal being as such. Nonbeing is mixed with being
in his moral self-affirmation as it is in his spiritual and
ontic self-affirmation. The awareness of this ambiguity is
the feeling of guilt. The judge who is oneself and who
stands against oneself, he who "knows with" (conscience) everything we do and are. gives a negative judgment, experienced by us as guilt. The anxiety of guilt
shows the same complex characteristics as the anxiety
about ontic and spiritual nonbeing. It is present in every
moment of moral self-awareness and can drive us toward

complete self-rejection, to the feeling of being condemned—not to an external punishment but to the despair
of having lost our destiny.

To avoid this extreme situation man tries to transform
the anxiety of guilt into moral action regardless of its imperfection and ambiguity. Courageously he takes nonbeing into his moral self-affirmation. This can happen in
two ways, according to the duality of the tragic and the
personal in man's situation, the first based on the contingencies of fate, the second on the responsibility of freedom. The first way can lead to a defiance of negative
judgments and the moral demands on which they are
based; the second way can lead to a moral rigor and the
self-satisfaction derived from it. In both of them—usually
called anomism and legalism—the anxiety of guilt lies in
the background and breaks again and again into the open,
producing the extreme situation of moral despair.

Nonbeing in a moral respect must be distinguished but
cannot be separated from ontic and spiritual nonbeing.
The anxiety of the one type is immanent in the anxieties
of the other types. The famous words of Paul about "sin
as the sting of death" point to the immanence of the anxiety of guilt within the fear of death. And the threat of
fate and death has always awakened and increased the
consciousness of guilt. The threat of moral nonbeing was
experienced in and through the threat of ontic nonbeing.
The contingencies of fate received moral interpretation:
fate executes the negative moral judgment by attacking
and perhaps destroying the ontic foundation of the mor-

ally rejected personality. The two forms of anxiety provoke and augment each other. In the same way spiritual and moral nonbeing are interdependent. Obedience to the moral norm, i.e. to one's own essential being, excludes emptiness and meaninglessness in their radical forms. If the spiritual contents have lost their power the self-affirmation of the moral personality is a way in which meaning can be rediscovered. The simple call to duty can save from emptiness, while the disintegration of the moral consciousness is an almost irresistible basis for the attack of spiritual nonbeing. On the other hand, existential doubt can undermine moral self-affirmation by throwing into the abyss of skepticism not only every moral principle but the meaning of moral self-affirmation as such. In this case the doubt is felt as guilt, while at the same time guilt is undermined by doubt.

THE MEANING OF DESPAIR

The three types of anxiety are interwoven in such a way that one of them gives the predominant color but all of them participate in the coloring of the state of anxiety. All of them and their underlying unity are existential, i.e. they are implied in the existence of man as man, his finitude, and his estrangement. They are fulfilled in the situation of despair to which all of them contribute. Despair is an ultimate or "boundary-line" situation. One cannot go beyond it. Its nature is indicated in the etymology of the word despair: without hope. No way out into the future appears. Nonbeing is felt as absolutely victorious. But there is a limit to its victory; nonbeing is *felt* as victorious, and feeling presupposes being. Enough being is left to feel the irresistible power of nonbeing, and this is the despair within the despair. The pain of despair is that a being is aware of itself as unable to affirm itself because of the power of nonbeing. Consequently it wants to surrender this awareness and its presupposition, the being which is aware. It wants to get rid of itself—and it cannot. Despair appears in the form of reduplication, as the desperate attempt to escape despair. If anxiety were only the anxiety of fate and death, voluntary death would be the way out of despair. The courage demanded would be the courage *not* to be. The final form of ontic self-affirmation would be the act of ontic self-negation.

But despair is also the despair about guilt and condemnation. And there is no way of escaping it, even by ontic self-negation. Suicide can liberate one from the anxiety of fate and death—as the Stoics knew. But it cannot liberate from the anxiety of guilt and condemnation, as the Christians know. This is a highly paradoxical statement, as paradoxical as the relation of the moral sphere to ontic existence generally. But it is a true statement, verified by those who have experienced fully the despair of condemnation. It is impossible to express the inescapable character of condemnation in ontic terms, that is in terms of imaginings about the "immortality of the soul." For every ontic statement must use the categories of finitude, and "immortality of the soul" would be the endless prolongation of finitude and of the despair of condemnation (a self-contradictory concept, for "finis" means "end"). The experience, therefore, that suicide is no way of escaping guilt must be understood in terms of the qualitative character of the moral demand, and of the qualitative character of its rejection. Guilt and condemnation are qualitatively, not quantitatively, infinite. They have an infinite weight and cannot be removed by a finite act of ontic self-negation. This makes despair desperate, that is, inescapable. There is "No Exit" from it (Sartre). The anxiety of emptiness and meaninglessness participates in both the ontic and the moral element in despair. Insofar as it is an expression of finitude it can be removed by ontic self-negation: This drives radical skepticism to suicide. Insofar as it is a consequence of moral disintegration it produces the same paradox as the moral element in despair: there is no ontic exit from it. This frustrates the suicidal trends in emptiness and meaninglessness. One is aware of their futility.

In view of this character of despair it is understandable that all human life can be interpreted as a continuous attempt to avoid despair. And this attempt is mostly successful. Extreme situations are not reached frequently and perhaps they are never reached by some people. The purpose of an analysis of such a situation is not to record ordinary human experiences but to show extreme possibilities in the light of which the ordinary situations must be understood. We are not always aware of our having to die, but in the light of the experience of our having to die our whole life is experienced differently. In the same way the anxiety which is despair is not always present.

But the rare occasions in which it is present determine the interpretation of existence as a whole.

PERIODS OF ANXIETY

The distinction of the three types of anxiety is supported by the history of Western civilization. We find that at the end of ancient civilization ontic anxiety is predominant, at the end of the Middle Ages moral anxiety, and at the end of the modern period spiritual anxiety. But in spite of the predominance of one type the others are also present and effective.

Enough has been said about the end of the ancient period and its anxiety of fate and death in connection with an analysis of Stoic courage. The sociological background is well known: the conflict of the imperial powers, Alexander's conquest of the East, the war between his followers, the conquest of West and East by republican Rome, the transformation of republican into imperial Rome through Caesar and Augustus, the tyranny of the post-Augustan emperors, the destruction of the independent city and nation states, the eradication of the former bearers of the aristocratic-democratic structure of society, the individual's feeling of being in the hands of powers, natural as well as political, which are completely beyond his control and calculation—all this produced a tremendous anxiety and the quest for courage to meet the threat of fate and death. At the same time the anxiety of emptiness and meaninglessness made it impossible for many people, especially of the educated classes, to find a basis for such courage. Ancient Skepticism from its very beginning in the Sophists united scholarly and existential elements. Skepticism in its late ancient form was despair about the possibility of right acting as well as right thinking. It drove people into the desert where the necessity for decisions, theoretical and practical, is reduced to a minimum. But most of those who experienced the anxiety of emptiness and the despair of meaninglessness tried to meet them with a cynical contempt of spiritual self-affirmation. Yet they could not hide the anxiety under skeptical arrogance. The anxiety of guilt and condemnation was effective in the groups who gathered in the mystery cults with their rites of expiation and purification. Sociologically these circles of the initiated were rather indefinite. In most of them even slaves were admitted. In them, however, as in the whole non-Jewish ancient world more the tragic than the personal guilt was experienced. Guilt is the pollution of the soul by the material realm or by demonic powers. Therefore the anxiety of guilt remains a secondary element, as does the anxiety of emptiness, within the dominating anxiety of fate and death.

Only the impact of the Jewish-Christian message changed this situation, and so radically that toward the end of the Middle Ages the anxiety of guilt and condemnation was decisive. If one period deserves the name of the "age of anxiety" it is the pre-Reformation and Reformation. The anxiety of condemnation symbolized as the "wrath of God" and intensified by the imagery of hell and purgatory drove people of the late Middle Ages to try various means of assuaging their anxiety: pilgrimages to holy places, if possible to Rome; ascetic exercises, sometimes of an extreme character; devotion to relics, often brought together in mass collections; acceptance of ecclesiastical punishments and the desire for indulgences; exaggerated participation in masses and penance, increase in prayers and alms. In short they asked ceaselessly: How can I appease the wrath of God, how can I attain divine mercy, the forgiveness of sin? This predominant form of anxiety embraced the other two forms. The personified figure of death appeared in painting, poetry, and preaching. But it was death and guilt together. Death and the devil were allied in the anxious imagination of the period. The anxiety of fate returned with the invasion of late antiquity. "Fortuna" became a preferred symbol in the art of the Renaissance, and even the Reformers were not free from astrological beliefs and fears. And the anxiety of fate was intensified by fear of demonic powers acting directly or through other human beings to cause illness, death, and all kinds of destruction. At the same time, fate was extended beyond death into the pre-ultimate state of purgatory and the ultimate states of hell or heaven. The darkness of ultimate destiny could not be removed; not even the Reformers were able to remove it, as their doctrine of predestination shows. In all these expressions the anxiety of fate appears as an element within the all-embracing anxiety of guilt and in the permanent awareness of the threat of condemnation.

The late Middle Ages was not a period of doubt; and

the anxiety of emptiness and loss of meaning appeared
only twice, both remarkable occasions, however, and important for the future. One was the Renaissance, when
theoretical skepticism was renewed and the question of
meaning haunted some of the most sensitive minds. In
Michelangelo's prophets and sibyls and in Shakespeare's
Hamlet there are indications of a potential anxiety of
meaninglessness. The other was in the demonic assaults
that Luther experienced, which were neither temptations
in the moral sense nor moments of despair about threatening condemnation, but moments when belief in his work
and message disappeared and no meaning remained. Similar experiences of the "desert" or the "night" of the soul
are frequent among mystics. It must be emphasized however that in all these cases the anxiety of guilt remained
predominant, and that only after the victory of humanism
and Enlightenment as the religious foundation of Western
society could anxiety about spiritual nonbeing become
dominant.

The sociological cause of the anxiety of guilt and condemnation that arose at the end of the Middle Ages is not
difficult to identify. In general one can say it was the dissolution of the protective unity of the religiously guided
medieval culture. More specifically there must be emphasized the rise of an educated middle class in the larger
cities, people who tried to have as their own experience
what had been merely an objective, hierarchically con-
trolled system of doctrines and sacraments. In this attempt,
however, they were driven to hidden or open conflict with

the Church, whose authority they still acknowledged. There must be emphasized the concentration of political power in the princes and their bureaucratic-military administration, which eliminated the independence of those lower in the feudal system. There must be emphasized the state absolutism which transformed the masses in city and country into "subjects" whose only duty was to work and to obey, without any power to resist the arbitrariness of the absolute rulers. There must be emphasized the economic catastrophes connected with early capitalism, such as the importation of gold from the New World, expropriation of the peasants, and so on. In all these often-described changes it is the conflict between the appearance of independent tendencies in all groups of society, on the one hand, and the rise of an absolutist concentration of power on the other that is largely responsible for the predominance of the anxiety of guilt. The irrational, commanding, absolute God of nominalism and the Reformation is partly shaped by the social, political, and spiritual absolutism of the period; and the anxiety created in turn by his image is partly an expression of the anxiety produced by the basic social conflict of the disintegrating Middle Ages.

The breakdown of absolutism, the development of liberalism and democracy, the rise of a technical civilization with its victory over all enemies and its own beginning disintegration—these are the sociological presupposition for the third main period of anxiety. In this the anxiety of emptiness and meaninglessness is dominant. We

are under the threat of spiritual nonbeing. The threats of
moral and ontic nonbeing are, of course, present, but they
are not independent and not controlling. This situation is
so fundamental to the question raised in this book that it
requires fuller analysis than the two earlier periods, and
the analysis must be correlated with the constructive solution (chapters 5 and 6).

It is significant that the three main periods of anxiety
appear at the end of an era. The anxiety which, in its different forms, is potentially present in every individual
becomes general if the accustomed structures of meaning,
power, belief, and order disintegrate. These structures,
as long as they are in force, keep anxiety bound within
a protective system of courage by participation. The individual who participates in the institutions and ways of
life of such a system is not liberated from his personal anxieties but he has means of overcoming them with well-
known methods. In periods of great changes these methods
no longer work. Conflicts between the old, which tries to
maintain itself, often with new means, and the new, which
deprives the old of its intrinsic power, produce anxiety
in all directions. Nonbeing, in such a situation, has a
double face, resembling two types of nightmare (which
are perhaps, expressions of an awareness of these two
faces). The one type is the anxiety of annihilating nar-
rowness, of the impossibility of escape and the horror of
being trapped. The other is the anxiety of annihilating
openness, of infinite, formless space into which one falls
without a place to fall upon. Social situations like those

described have the character both of a trap without exit and of an empty, dark, and unknown void. Both faces of the same reality arouse the latent anxiety of every individual who looks at them. Today most of us do look at them.

THE NATURE OF PATHOLOGICAL ANXIETY

We have discussed three forms of existential anxiety, an anxiety which is given with human existence itself. Non-existential anxiety, which is the result of contingent occurrences in human life, has been mentioned only in passing. It is now time to deal with it systematically. An ontology of anxiety and courage such as is developed in this book naturally cannot attempt to present a psychotherapeutic theory of neurotic anxiety. Many theories are under discussion today; and some of the leading psychotherapists, notably Freud himself, have developed different interpretations. There is, however, one common denominator in all the theories: anxiety is the awareness of unsolved conflicts between structural elements of the personality, as for instance conflicts between unconscious drives and repressive norms, between different drives trying to dominate the center of the personality, between imaginary worlds and the experience of the real world, between trends toward greatness and perfection and the experience of one's smallness and imperfection, between the desire to be accepted by other people or society or the universe and the experience of being rejected, between the will to be and the seemingly intolerable burden of being which evokes the open or hidden desire not to be. All these conflicts, whether unconscious, subconscious, or conscious, whether unadmitted or admitted, make themselves felt in sudden or lasting stages of anxiety. Usually one of these explanations of anxiety is considered the fundamental one. A search for the basic anxiety, not in cultural but in psychological terms, is made by practical and theoretical analysts. But in most of these attempts a criterion of what is basic and what is derived seems to be lacking. Each of these explanations points to actual symptoms and fundamental structures. But because of the variety of the observed material the elevation of one part of it to central significance is usually not convincing. There is still another reason for the psychotherapeutic theory of anxiety being in a confused state in spite of all its brilliant insights. It is the lack of a clear distinction between existential and pathological anxiety, and between the main forms of existential anxiety. This cannot be made by depth-psychological analysis alone; it is a matter of ontology. Only in the light of an ontological understanding of human nature can the body of material provided by psychology and sociology be organized into a consistent and comprehensive theory of anxiety.

Pathological anxiety is a state of existential anxiety under special conditions. The general character of these conditions depends on the relation of anxiety to self-affirmation and courage. We have seen that anxiety tends to become fear in order to have an object with which courage can deal. Courage does not remove anxiety. Since anxiety is existential, it cannot be removed. But courage takes the anxiety of nonbeing into itself. Courage is self-affirmation "in spite of," namely in spite of nonbeing. He who acts courageously takes, in his self-affirmation, the anxiety of nonbeing upon himself. Both prepositions, "into" and "upon," are metaphoric and point to anxiety as an element within the total structure of self-affirmation, the element which gives self-affirmation the quality of "in spite of" and transforms it into courage. Anxiety turns us toward courage, because the other alternative is despair. Courage resists despair by taking anxiety into itself.

This analysis gives the key to understanding pathological anxiety. He who does not succeed in taking his anxiety courageously upon himself can succeed in avoiding the extreme situation of despair by escaping into neurosis. He still affirms himself but on a limited scale. *Neurosis is the way of avoiding nonbeing by avoiding being.* In the neurotic state self-affirmation is not lacking; it can indeed be very strong and emphasized. But the self which is affirmed is a reduced one. Some or many of its potentialities are not admitted to actualization, because actualization of being implies the acceptance of nonbeing and its anxiety. He who is not capable of a powerful self-affirmation in spite of the anxiety of nonbeing is forced into a weak, reduced self-affirmation. He affirms something which is less than his essential or potential being. He surrenders a part of his potentialities in order to save what is left. This structure explains the ambiguities of the neurotic character. The neurotic is more sensitive than the average man to the threat of nonbeing. And since nonbeing opens up the mystery of being (see Chapter 6) he can be more creative than the average. This limited extensiveness of self-affirmation can be balanced by greater intensity, but by an intensity which is narrowed to a special point accompanied by a distorted relation to reality as a whole. Even if pathological anxiety has psychotic traits, creative moments can appear. There are sufficient examples of this fact in the biographies of creative men. And as the example of the demoniacs of the New Testament shows, people far below the average can have flashes of insight which the masses and even the disciples of Jesus do not have: the profound anxiety produced by the presence of Jesus reveals to them in a very early stage of his appearance his messianic character. The history of human culture proves that again and again neurotic anxiety breaks through the walls of ordinary self-affirmation and opens up levels of reality which are normally hidden.

This however brings us to the question whether the normal self-affirmation of the average man is not even more limited than the pathological self-affirmation of the neurotic, and consequently whether the state of pathological anxiety and self-affirmation is not the ordinary state of man. It has often been said that there are neurotic elements in everybody and that the difference between the sick and the healthy mind is only a quantitative one. One could support this theory by referring to the psychosomatic character of most diseases and to the presence of elements of illness in even the most healthy body. Insofar as the psychosomatic correlation is valid this would indicate the presence of elements of illness also in the healthy mind. Is there then a distinction between the neurotic and the average mind which is conceptually sharp even if reality has many transitions?

The difference between the neurotic and the healthy (although potentially neurotic) personality is the following: the neurotic personality, on the basis of his greater sensitivity to nonbeing and consequently of his profounder anxiety, has settled down to a fixed, though limited and unrealistic, self-affirmation. This is, so to speak, the castle to which he has retired and which he defends with all means of psychological resistance against attack, be it from the side of reality or from the side of the analyst. And this resistance is not without some instinctive wisdom. The neurotic is aware of the danger of a situation in which his unrealistic self-affirmation is broken down and *no* realistic self-affirmation takes its place. The danger is either that he will fall back into another and much better defended neurosis or that with the breakdown of his limited self-affirmation he will fall into an unlimited despair.

The situation is different in the case of the normal self-affirmation of the average personality. That also is fragmentary. The average person keeps himself away from the extreme situations by dealing courageously with concrete objects of fear. He usually is not aware of nonbeing and anxiety in the depth of his personality. But his fragmentary self-affirmation is not fixed and defended against an overwhelming threat of anxiety. He is adjusted to reality in many more directions than the neurotic. He is superior in extensity, but he is lacking in the intensity which can make the neurotic creative. His anxiety does not drive him to the construction of imaginary worlds. He affirms himself in unity with those parts of reality which he encounters; and they are not definitively circumscribed. This is what makes him healthy in comparison with the neurotic. The neurotic is sick and needs healing because of the conflict in which he finds himself with reality. In this conflict he is hurt by the reality which permanently penetrates the castle of his defense and the imaginary world behind it. His limited and fixed self-affirmation both preserves him from an intolerable impact of anxiety and destroys him by turning him against reality and reality against him, and by producing another intolerable attack of anxiety. Pathological anxiety, in spite of its creative potentialities, is illness and danger and must be healed by being taken into a courage to be which is extensive as well as intensive.

There is a moment in which the self-affirmation of the average man becomes neurotic: when changes of the reality to which he is adjusted threaten the fragmentary courage with which he has mastered the accustomed objects of fear. If this happens—and it often happens in critical periods of history—the self-affirmation becomes pathological. The dangers connected with the change, the unknown character of the things to come, the darkness of the future make the average man a fanatical defender of the established order. He defends it as compulsively as the neurotic defends the castle of his imaginary world. He loses his comparative openness to reality, he experiences an unknown depth of anxiety. But if he is not able to take this anxiety into his self-affirmation his anxiety turns into neurosis. This is the explanation of the mass neuroses which usually appear at the end of an era (see the previous chapter about the three periods of anxiety in Western history). In such periods existential anxiety is mixed with neurotic anxiety to such a degree that historians and analysts are unable to draw the boundary lines sharply. When, for example, does the anxiety of condemnation which underlies asceticism become pathological? Is the anxiety about the demonic *always* neurotic or even psychotic? To what degree are present-day Existentialist descriptions of man's predicament caused by neurotic anxiety?

Anxiety, Religion, and Medicine

Such questions prompt a consideration of the way of healing over which two faculties, the theological and the medical, struggle with each other. Medicine, above all psychotherapy and psychoanalysis, often claims that healing anxiety is its task because all anxiety is pathological. Healing consists in removing anxiety altogether, for anxiety is sickness, mostly in a psychosomatic, sometimes only in a psychological sense. All forms of anxiety can be healed, and since there is no ontological root of anxiety there is no existential anxiety. Medical insight and medical help—this is the conclusion—are the way to the courage to be; the medical profession is the only healing profession. Although this extreme position is taken by an ever-decreasing number of physicians and psychotherapists it remains important from the theoretical point of view. It includes a decision about the nature of man which must be made explicit, in spite of the positivistic resistance to ontology. The psychiatrist who asserts that anxiety is always pathological cannot deny the *potentiality* of illness in human *nature*, and he must account for the facts of finitude, doubt, and guilt in every human being; he must, in terms of his own presupposition, account for the universality of anxiety. He cannot avoid the question of human nature since in practicing his profession he cannot avoid the distinction between health and illness, existential and pathological anxiety. This is why more and more representatives of medicine generally and psychotherapy specifically ask for the cooperation with the philosophers and theologians. And it is why through this cooperation a practice of "counseling" has developed which is, like every attempted synthesis, dangerous as well as significant for the future. The medical faculty needs a doctrine of man in order to fulfill its theoretical task; and it cannot have a doctrine of man without the permanent cooperation of all those faculties whose central object is man. The medical profession has the purpose of helping man in some of his existential problems, those which usually are called diseases. But it cannot help man without the permanent cooperation of all other professions whose purpose is to help man as man. Both the doctrines about man and the help given to man are a matter of cooperation from many points of view. Only in this way is it possible to understand and to actualize man's power of being, his essential self-affirmation, his courage to be.

The theological faculty and the practical ministry face the same problem. In all their teaching and practice a doctrine of man and with it an ontology is presupposed. This is why theology in most periods of its history has sought the assistance of philosophy in spite of frequent theological or popular protests (which are the counter-part to the protests of empirical medicine against the phi-losophers of medicine). However successful the escape from philosophy might have been, in regard to the doc-trine of man it was plainly unsuccessful. Therefore in the interpretation of human existence theology and medi-cine unavoidably joined philosophy, whether they were conscious of it or not. And in joining philosophy they joined each other even if their understanding of man went toward opposite directions. Today the theological as well as the medical faculty is aware of this situation and its theoretical and practical implications. Theologians and ministers eagerly seek collaboration with medical men, and many forms of occasional or institutionalized coopera-tion result. But the lack of an ontological analysis of anx-iety and of a sharp distinction between existential and pathological anxiety has prevented as many ministers and theologians as physicians and psychotherapists from entering this alliance. Since they do not see the difference they are unwilling to look at neurotic anxiety as they look at bodily disease, namely as an object of medical help. But if one preaches ultimate courage to somebody who is pathologically fixed to a limited self-affirmation, the content of the preaching is either resisted compulsively or—even worse—is taken into the castle of self-defense as another implement for avoiding the encounter with reality. Much enthusiastic reaction to religious appeal must be considered with suspicion from the point of view of a realistic self-affirmation. Much courage to be, created by religion, is nothing else than the desire to limit one's own being and to strengthen this limitation through the power of religion. And even if religion does not lead to or does not directly support pathological self-reduction, it can reduce the openness of man to reality, above all to the reality which is himself. In this way religion can protect and feed a potentially neurotic state. These dangers must be realized by the minister and met with the help of the physician and psychotherapist.

Some principles for the cooperation of the theological and medical faculties in dealing with anxiety can be derived from our ontological analysis. The basic principle is that existential anxiety in its three main forms is not the concern of the physician *as* physician, although he must be fully aware of it; and, conversely, that neurotic anxiety in all its forms is not the concern of the minister *as* minister, although he must be fully aware of it. The minister raises the question concerning a courage to be which takes existential anxiety into itself. The physician raises the question concerning a courage to be in which the neurotic anxiety is removed. But neurotic anxiety is, as our ontological analysis has shown, the inability to take one's existential anxiety upon oneself. Therefore the ministerial function comprehends both itself and the medical function. Neither of these functions is absolutely bound to those who exercise it professionally. The physician, especially the psychotherapist, can implicitly communicate courage to be and the power of taking existential anxiety upon oneself. He does not become a minister in doing so and he never should try to replace the minister, but he can become a helper to ultimate self-affirmation, thus performing a ministerial function. Conversely the minister or anyone else can become a medical helper. He does not become a physician and no minister should aspire to become one *as* a minister although he may radiate healing power for mind and body and help to remove neurotic anxiety.

If this basic principle is applied to the three main forms of existential anxiety other principles can be derived. The anxiety of fate and death produces nonpathological strivings for security. Large sections of man's civilization serve the purpose of giving him safety against the attacks of fate and death. He realizes that no absolute and no final security is possible; he also realizes that life demands again and again the courage to surrender some or even all security for the sake of full self-affirmation. Nevertheless he tries to reduce the power of fate and the threat of death as much as possible. Pathological anxiety about fate and death impels toward a security which is comparable to the security of a prison. He who lives in this prison is unable to leave the security given to him by his self-imposed limitations. But these limitations are not based on a full awareness of reality. Therefore the security of the neurotic is unrealistic. He fears what is not to be feared and he feels to be safe what is not safe. The anxiety which he is not able to take upon himself produces images having no basis in reality, but it recedes in the face of things which should be feared. That is, one avoids particular dangers, although they are hardly real, and suppresses the awareness of having to die although this is an ever-present reality. *Misplaced* fear is a consequence of the pathological form of the anxiety of fate and death.

The same structure can be observed in the pathological forms of the anxiety of guilt and condemnation. The normal, existential anxiety of guilt drives the person toward attempts to avoid this anxiety (usually called the uneasy conscience) by avoiding guilt. Moral self-discipline and habits will produce moral perfection although one remains aware that they cannot remove the imperfection which is implied in man's existential situation, his estrangement from his true being. Neurotic anxiety does the same thing but in a limited, fixed, and unrealistic way. The anxiety of becoming guilty, the horror of feeling condemned, are so strong that they make responsible decisions and any kind of moral action almost impossible. But since decisions and actions cannot be avoided they are reduced to a minimum which, however, is considered absolutely perfect; and the sphere where they take place is defended against any provocation to transcend it. Here also the separation from reality has the consequence that the consciousness of guilt is misplaced. The moralistic self-defense of the neurotic makes him see guilt where there is no guilt or where one is guilty only in a very indirect way. Yet the awareness of real guilt and the self-condemnation which is identical with man's existential self-estrangement are repressed, because the courage which could take them into itself is lacking.

The pathological forms of the anxiety of emptiness and meaninglessness show similar characteristics. Existential anxiety of doubt drives the person toward the creation of certitude in systems of meaning, which are supported by tradition and authority. In spite of the element of doubt which is implied in man's finite spirituality, and in spite of the threat of meaninglessness implied in man's estrangement, anxiety is reduced by these ways of producing and preserving certitude. Neurotic anxiety builds a narrow castle of certitude which can be defended and is defended with the utmost tenacity. Man's power of asking is prevented from becoming actual in this sphere, and if there is a danger of its becoming actualized by questions asked from the outside he reacts with a fanatical rejection. However the castle of undoubted certitude is not built on the rock of reality. The inability of the neurotic to have a full encounter with reality makes his doubts as well as his certitudes unrealistic. He puts both in the wrong place. He doubts what is practically above doubt and he is certain where doubt is adequate. Above all, he does not admit the question of meaning in its universal and radical sense. The question is in him, as it is in every man as man under the conditions of existential estrangement. But he cannot admit it because he is without the courage to take the anxiety of emptiness or doubt and meaninglessness upon himself.

The analyses of pathological in relation to existential anxiety have brought out the following principles: 1. Existential anxiety has an ontological character and cannot be removed but must be taken into the courage to be. 2. Pathological anxiety is the consequence of the failure of the self to take the anxiety upon itself. 3. Pathological anxiety leads to self-affirmation on a limited, fixed, and unrealistic basis and to a compulsory defense of this basis. 4. Pathological anxiety, in relation to the anxiety of fate and death, produces an unrealistic security; in relation to the anxiety of guilt and condemnation, an unrealistic perfection; in relation to the anxiety of doubt and meaninglessness, an unrealistic certitude. 5. Pathological anxiety, once established, is an object of medical healing. Existential anxiety is an object of priestly help. Neither the medical nor the priestly function is bound to its vocational representatives: the minister may be a healer and the psychotherapist a priest, and each human being may be both in relation to the "neighbor." But the functions should not be confused and the representatives should not try to replace each other. The goal of both of them is helping

men to reach full self-affirmation, to attain the courage
to be.

VITALITY AND COURAGE

Anxiety and courage have a psychosomatic character.
They are biological as well as psychological. From the
biological point of view one would say that fear and anxiety are the guardians, indicating the threat of nonbeing
to a living being and producing movements of protection
and resistance to this threat. Fear and anxiety must be
considered as expressions of what one could call: "self-
affirmation on its guard." Without the anticipating fear
and the compelling anxiety no finite being would be able
to exist. Courage, in this view, is the readiness to take upon
oneself negatives, anticipated by fear, for the sake of a
fuller positivity. Biological self-affirmation implies the acceptance of want, toil, insecurity, pain, possible destruction. Without this self-affirmation life could not be preserved or increased. The more vital strength a being has
the more it is able to affirm itself in spite of the dangers
announced by fear and anxiety. However, it would contradict their biological function if courage disregarded
their warnings and prompted actions of a directly self-
destructive character. This is the truth in Aristotle's doctrine of courage as the right mean between cowardice and
temerity. Biological self-affirmation needs a balance between courage and fear. Such a balance is present in all
living beings which are able to preserve and increase their
being. If the warnings of fear no longer have an effect or

if the dynamics of courage have lost their power, life vanishes. The drive for security, perfection, and certitude to which we have referred is biologically necessary. But it becomes biologically destructive if the risk of insecurity, imperfection, and uncertainty is avoided. Conversely, a risk which has a realistic foundation in our self and our world is biologically demanded, while it is self-destructive without such a foundation. Life, in consequence, includes both fear and courage as elements of a life process in a changing but essentially established balance. As long as life has such a balance it is able to resist nonbeing. Unbalanced fear and unbalanced courage destroy the life whose preservation and increase are the function of the balance of fear and courage.

A life process which shows this balance and with it power of being has, in biological terms, vitality, i.e. life power. The right courage therefore must, like the right fear, be understood as the expression of perfect vitality. The courage to be is a function of vitality. Diminishing vitality consequently entails diminishing courage. To strengthen vitality means to strengthen the courage to be. Neurotic individuals and neurotic periods are lacking in vitality. Their biological substance has disintegrated. They have lost the power of full self-affirmation, of the courage to be. Whether this happens or not is the result of biological processes, it is biological fate. The periods of a diminished courage to be are periods of biological weakness in the individual and in history. The three main periods of unbalanced anxiety are periods of reduced vitality; they are ends of an era and could be overcome only by the rise of vitally powerful groups that replaced the vitally disintegrated groups.

Up to this point we have given the biological argument without criticism. We now must examine the validity of its different steps. The first question to be asked refers to the difference between fear and anxiety as developed earlier. There can be no doubt that fear which is directed toward a definite object has the biological function of announcing threats of nonbeing and provoking measures of protection and resistance. But one must ask: Is the same true of anxiety? Our biological argument has used the term fear predominantly, the term anxiety only exceptionally. This was done intentionally. For, biologically speaking, anxiety is more destructive than protective. While fear can lead to measures that deal with the objects of fear, anxiety cannot do so because it has no objects. The fact, already referred to, that life tries to transform anxiety into fear shows that anxiety is biologically useless and cannot be explained in terms of life protection. It produces self-defying forms of behavior. Anxiety therefore by its very nature transcends the biological argument.

The second point to be made concerns the concept of vitality. The meaning of vitality has become an important problem since fascism and nazism transferred the theoretical emphasis on vitality into political systems which in the name of vitality attacked most of the values of the Western world. In Plato's *Laches* the relation of courage and vitality is discussed in terms of whether animals have courage. Much can be said for an affirmative answer: the balance between fear and courage is well developed in the animal realm. Animals are warned by fear, but under special conditions they disregard their fear and risk pain and annihilation for the sake of those who are a part of their own self-affirmation, e.g., their descendants or their flock. But in spite of these obvious facts Plato rejects animal courage. Naturally so, for if courage is the knowledge of what to avoid and what to dare, courage cannot be separated from man as a rational being.

Vitality, power of life, is correlated to the kind of life to which it gives power. The power of man's life cannot be seen separately from what the medieval philosophers called "intentionality," the relation to meanings. Man's vitality is as great as his intentionality; they are interdependent. This makes man the most vital of all beings. He can transcend any given situation in any direction and this possibility drives him to create beyond himself. Vitality is the power of creating beyond oneself without losing oneself. The more power of creating beyond itself a being has the more vitality it has. The world of technical creations is the most conspicuous expression of man's vitality and its infinite superiority over animal vitality. Only man has complete vitality because he alone has complete intentionality.

We have defined intentionality as "being directed toward meaningful contents." Man lives "in" meanings, in that which is valid logically, esthetically, ethically, religiously. His subjectivity is impregnated with objectivity. In every encounter with reality the structures of self and world are interdependently present. The most fundamental expression of this fact is the language which gives man the power to abstract from the concretely given and, after having abstracted from it, to return to it, to interpret and transform it. The most vital being is the being which has the word and is by the word liberated from bondage to the given. In every encounter with reality man is already beyond this encounter. He knows about it, he compares it, he is tempted by other possibilities, he anticipates the future as he remembers the past. This is his freedom, and in this freedom the power of his life consists. It is the source of his vitality.

If the correlation between vitality and intentionality is rightly understood one can accept the biological interpretation of courage within the limits of its validity. Certainly courage is a function of vitality, but vitality is not something which can be separated from the totality of man's being, his language, his creativity, his spiritual life, his ultimate concern. One of the unfortunate consequences of the intellectualization of man's spiritual life was that the word "spirit" was lost and replaced by mind or intellect, and that the element of vitality which is present in "spirit" was separated and interpreted as an independent biological force. Man was divided into a bloodless intellect and a meaningless vitality. The middle ground between them, the spiritual soul in which vitality and intentionality are united, was dropped. At the end of this development it was easy for a reductive naturalism to derive self-affirmation and courage from a merely biological vitality. But in man nothing is "merely biological" as nothing is "merely spiritual." Every cell of his body participates in his freedom and spirituality, and every act of his spiritual creativity is nourished by his vital dynamics.

This unity was presupposed in the Greek word *aretė*. It can be translated by virtue, but only if the moralistic connotations of "virtue" are removed. The Greek term combines strength and value, the power of being and the fulfillment of meaning. The *aretés* is the bearer of high values, and the ultimate test of his aretė is his readiness to sacrifice himself for them. His courage expresses his intentionality as much as his vitality. It is spiritually formed vitality which makes him aretés. Behind this terminology stands the judgment of the ancient world that courage is noble. The pattern of the courageous man is not the self-wasting barbarian whose vitality is not fully human but the educated Greek who knows the anxiety of nonbeing because he knows the value of being. It may be added that the Latin word *virtus* and its derivatives, the Renaissance-Italian *virtu* and the Renaissance-English "virtue," have a meaning similar to aretė. They designate the quality of those who unite masculine strength *(virtus)* with moral nobility. Vitality and intentionality are united in this ideal of human perfection, which is equally removed from barbarism and from moralism.

In the light of these considerations one could reply to

the biologistic argument that it falls short of what classical antiquity had called courage. Vitalism in the sense of a separation of the vital from the intentional necessarily reestablishes the barbarian as the ideal of courage. Although this is done in the interest of science it expresses—usually against the will of its naturalistic defenders—a prehumanist attitude and can, if used by demagogues, produce the barbaric ideal of courage as it appeared in fascism and nazism. "Pure" vitality in man is never pure but always distorted, because man's power of life is his freedom and the spirituality in which vitality and intentionality are united.

There is, however, a third point on which the biological interpretation of courage demands evaluation. It is the answer biologism gives to the question of where the courage to be originates. The biological argument answers: in the vital power which is a natural gift, a matter of biological fate. This is very similar to the ancient and medieval answers in which a combination of biological and historical fate, the aristocratic situation, was considered the condition favorable for the growth of courage. In both cases courage is a possibility dependent not on will power or insight but on a gift which precedes action. The tragic view of the early Greeks and the deterministic view of modern naturalism agree in this point: the power of "self-affirmation in spite of," i.e. the courage to be, is a matter of fate. This does not prohibit a moral valuation but it prohibits a moralistic valuation of courage: one cannot command the courage to be and one cannot gain it by obeying a command. Religiously speaking, it is a matter of grace. As often happens in the history of thought, naturalism has paved the way to a new understanding of grace, while idealism has prevented such understanding. From this point of view the biological argument is very important and must be taken seriously, especially by ethics, in spite of the distortions of the concept of vitality in biological as well as in political vitalism. The truth of the vitalistic interpretation of ethics is grace. Courage as grace is a result and a question.

BEING, INDIVIDUALIZATION, AND PARTICIPATION

This is not the place to develop a doctrine of the basic ontological structure and its constituent elements. Something of it has been done in my *Systematic Theology*, Vol. 1, Part I. The present discussion must refer to the assertions of those chapters without repeating their arguments. Ontological principles have a polar character according to the basic polar structure of being, that of self and world. The first polar elements are individualization and participation. Their bearing on the problem of courage is obvious, if courage is defined as the self-affirmation of being in spite of nonbeing. If we ask: what is the subject of this self-affirmation, we must answer: the individual self which participates in the world, i.e. the structural universe of being. Man's self-affirmation has two sides which are distinguishable but not separable: one is the affirmation of the self as a self; that is of a separated, self-centered, individualized, incomparable, free, self-determining self. This is what one affirms in every act of self-affirmation. This is what one defends against nonbeing and affirms courageously by taking nonbeing upon oneself. The threatened loss of it is the essence of anxiety, and the awareness of concrete threats to it is the essence of fear. Ontological self-affirmation precedes all differences of metaphysical, ethical, or religious definition of the self. Ontological self-affirmation is neither natural nor spiritual, neither good nor evil, neither immanent nor transcendent. These differences are possible only because of the underlying ontological self-affirmation of the self as self. In the same way the concepts which characterize the individual self lie below the differences of valuation: separation is not estrangement, self-centeredness is not selfishness, self-determination is not sinfulness. They are structural descriptions and the condition of both love and hate, condemnation and salvation. It is time to end the bad theological usage of jumping with moral indignation on every word in which the syllable "self" appears. Even moral indignation would not exist without a centered self and ontological self-affirmation.

The subject of self-affirmation is the centered self. As centered self it is an individualized self. It can be destroyed but it cannot be divided: each of its parts has the mark of this and no other self. Nor can it be exchanged: its self-affirmation is directed to itself as this unique, unrepeatable, and irreplaceable individual. The theological assertion that every human soul has an infinite value is a consequence of the ontological self-affirmation as an indivisible, unexchangeable self. It can be called "the courage to be as oneself."

But the self is self only because it has a world, a struc-

tured universe, to which it belongs and from which it is
separated at the same time. Self and world are correlated,
and so are individualization and participation. For this is
just what participation means: being a part of something
from which one is, at the same time, separated. Literally,
participation means "taking part." This can be used in a
threefold sense. It can be used in the sense of "sharing,"
as, for instance, sharing a room; or in the sense of "having in common," as Plato speaks of the *methexis* ("having
with"), the participation of the individual in the universal;
or it can be used in the sense of "being a part," for instance
of a political movement. In all these cases participation is
a partial identity and a partial nonidentity. A part of a
whole is not identical with the whole to which it belongs.
But the whole is what it is only with the part. The relation
of the body and its limbs is the most obvious example. The
self is a part of the world which it has as its world. The
world would not be what it is without *this* individual self.
One says that somebody is identified with a movement.
This participation makes his being and the being of the
movement partly the same. To understand the highly
dialectical nature of participation it is necessary to think
in terms of power instead of in terms of things. The partial
identity of definitely separated things cannot be thought
of. But the power of being can be shared by different individuals. The power of being of a state can be shared by
all its citizens, and in an outstanding way by its rulers. Its
power is partly their power, although its power transcends their power and their power transcends its power.

The identity of participation is an identity in the power of being. In this sense the power of being of the individual self is partly identical with the power of being of his world, and conversely.

For the concepts of self-affirmation and courage this means that the self-affirmation of the self as an individual self always includes the affirmation of the power of being in which the self participates. The self affirms itself as participant in the power of a group, of a movement, of essences, of the power of being as such. Self-affirmation, if it is done in spite of the threat of nonbeing, is the courage to be. But it is not the courage to be as oneself, it is the "courage to be as a part."

The phrase "courage to be as a part" presents a difficulty. While it obviously demands courage to be as oneself, the will to be as a part seems to express the lack of courage, namely the desire to live under the protection of a larger whole. Not courage but weakness seems to induce us to affirm ourselves as a part. But being as a part points to the fact that self-affirmation necessarily includes the affirmation of oneself as "participant," and that this side of our self-affirmation is threatened by nonbeing as much as the other side, the affirmation of the self as an individual self. We are threatened not only with losing our individual selves but also with losing participation in our world. Therefore self-affirmation as a part requires courage as much as does self-affirmation as oneself. It is *one* courage which takes a double threat of nonbeing into itself. The courage to be is essentially always the courage to be as a part and the courage to be as oneself, in interdependence. The courage to be as a part is an integral element of the courage to be as oneself, and the courage to be as oneself is an integral element of the courage to be as a part. But under the conditions of human finitude and estrangement that which is essentially united becomes existentially split. The courage to be as a part separates itself from unity with the courage to be as oneself, and conversely; and both disintegrate in their isolation. The anxiety they had taken into themselves is unloosed and becomes destructive. This situation determines our further procedure: we shall deal first with manifestations of the courage to be as a part, then with manifestations of the courage to be as oneself, and in the third place we shall consider a courage in which the two sides are reunited.

COLLECTIVIST AND SEMICOLLECTIVIST MANIFES-TATIONS OF THE COURAGE TO BE AS A PART

The courage to be as a part is the courage to affirm one's own being by participation. One participates in the world to which one belongs and from which one is at the same time separated. But participating in the world becomes real through participation in those sections of it which constitute one's own life. The world as a whole is potential, not actual. Those sections are actual with which one is partially identical. The more self-relatedness a being has the more it is able, according to the polar structure of reality, to participate. Man as the completely centered being or as a person can participate in everything, but he participates through that section of the world which makes him a person. Only in the continuous encounter with other persons does the person become and remain a person. The place of this encounter is the community. Man's participation in nature is direct, insofar as he is a definite part of nature through his bodily existence. His participation in nature is indirect and mediated through the community insofar as he transcends nature by knowing and shaping it. Without language there are no universals; without universals no transcending of nature and no relation to it as nature. But language is communal, not individual. The section of reality in which one participates immediately is the community to which one belongs. Through it and only through it participation in the world as a whole and in all its parts is mediated.

Therefore he who has the courage to be as a part has the courage to affirm himself as a part of the community in which he participates. His self-affirmation is a part of the self-affirmation of the social groups which constitute the society to which he belongs. This seems to imply that there is a collective and not only an individual self-affirmation, and that the collective self-affirmation is threatened by nonbeing, producing collective anxiety, which is met by collective courage. One could say the subject of this anxiety and this courage is a we-self as against the ego-selves who are parts of it. But such an enlargement of the meaning of "self" must be rejected. Self-hood is self-centeredness. Yet there is no center in a group in the sense in which it exists in a person. There may be a central power, a king, a president, a dictator. He may be able to impose his will on the group. But it is not the group which decides if he decides, though the group may follow. Therefore it is neither adequate to speak of a we-self nor useful to employ the terms collective anxiety and collective courage. When describing the three periods of anxiety, we pointed out that masses of people were overtaken by a special type of anxiety because many of them experienced the same anxiety-producing situation and because outbreaks of anxiety are always contagious. There is no collective anxiety save an anxiety which has overtaken many or all members of a group and has been intensified or changed by becoming universal. The same is true of what is wrongly called collective courage. There is no entity "we-self" as the subject of courage. There are selves who participate in a group and whose character is partly determined by this participation. The assumed we-self is a common quality of ego-selves within a group. The courage to be as a part is like all forms of courage, a quality of individual selves.

A collectivist society is one in which the existence and life of the individual are determined by the existence and institutions of the group. In collectivist societies the courage of the individual is the courage to be as a part. Looking at so-called primitive societies one finds typical forms of anxiety and typical institutions in which courage expresses itself. The individual members of the group develop equal anxieties and fears. And they use the same methods of developing courage and fortitude which are prescribed by traditions and institutions. This courage is the courage which every member of the group is supposed to have. In many tribes the courage to take pain upon oneself is the test of full membership in the group, and the courage to take death upon oneself is a lasting test in the life of most groups. The courage of him who stands these tests is the courage to be as a part. He affirms himself through the group in which he participates. The potential anxiety of losing himself in the group is not actualized, because the identification with the group is complete. Nonbeing in the form of the threat of loss of self in the group has not yet appeared. Self-affirmation within a group includes the courage to accept guilt and its consequences as public guilt, whether one is oneself responsible or whether somebody else is. It is a problem of the group which has to be expiated for the sake of the group, and the methods of punishment and satisfaction requested by the group are accepted by the individual. Individual guilt consciousness exists only as the consciousness of a deviation from the institutions and rules of the collective. Truth and meaning are embodied in the traditions and symbols of the group, and there is no autonomous asking and doubt. But even in a primitive collective, as in every human community, there are outstanding members, the bearers of the traditions and leaders of the future. They must have sufficient distance in order to judge and to change. They must take responsibility and ask questions. This unavoidably produces individual doubt and personal guilt. Nevertheless, the predominant pattern is the courage to be as a part in all members of the primitive group.

In the first chapter, while dealing with the concept of courage, I referred to the Middle Ages and its aristocratic interpretation of courage. The courage of the Middle Ages as of every feudal society is basically the courage to be as a part. The so-called realistic philosophy of the Middle Ages is a philosophy of participation. It presupposes that universals logically and collectives actually have more reality than the individual. The particular (literally: being a small part) has its power of being by participation in the universal. The self-affirmation expressed for instance in the self-respect of the individual is self-affirmation as follower of a feudal lord or as the member of a guild or as the student in an academic corporation or as a bearer of a special function like that of a craft or a trade or a profession. But the Middle Ages, in spite of all primitive elements, is not primitive. Two things happened in the ancient world which separate medieval collectivism definitively from primitive collectivism. One was the discovery of personal guilt—called by the prophets guilt before God: the decisive step to the personalization of religion and culture. The other was the beginning of autonomous question-asking in Greek philosophy, the decisive step to the problematization of culture and religion. Both elements were transmitted to the medieval nations by the Church. With them went the anxiety of guilt and condemnation and the anxiety of doubt and meaninglessness. As in later antiquity this could have led to a situation in which the courage to be as oneself was necessary. But the Church gave an antidote against the threat of anxiety and despair, namely itself, its traditions, its sacraments, its education, and its authority. The anxiety of guilt was taken into the courage to be as a part of the sacramental community. The anxiety of doubt was taken into the courage to be as a part of the community in which revelation and reason are united. In this way the medieval courage to be was, in spite of its difference from primitive collectivism, the courage to be as a part. The tension created by this situation is theoretically expressed in the attack of nominalism on medieval realism and the permanent conflict between them. Nominalism attributes ultimate reality to the individual and would have led much earlier than it actually did to a dissolution of the medieval system of participation if the immensely strengthened authority of the Church had not delayed it.

In religious practice the same tension was expressed in the duality of the sacraments of the mass and of penance. The former mediated the objective power of salvation in which everybody was supposed to participate, if possible by being present at its daily performance. In consequence of this universal participation guilt and grace were felt not only as personal but also as communal. The punishment of the sinner had representative character in such a way that the whole community suffered with him. And the liberation of the sinner from punishment on earth and in purgatory was partly dependent on the representative holiness of the saints and the love of those who made sacrifices for his liberation. Nothing is more characteristic of the medieval system of participation than this mutual representation. The courage to be as a part and to take upon oneself the anxieties of nonbeing is embodied in medieval institutions as it was in primitive forms of life. But medieval semicollectivism came to an end when the anticollectivist pole, represented by the sacrament of penance, came to the fore. The principle that only "contrition," the personal and total acceptance of judgment and grace, can make the objective sacraments effective was impelling toward reduction and even exclusion of the objective element, of representation and participation. In the act of contrition everybody stands alone before God; and it was hard for the Church to mediate this element with the objective one. Finally it proved impossible and the system disintegrated. At the same time the nominalistic tradition became powerful and liberated itself from the heteronomy of the Church. In Reformation and Renaissance the medieval courage to be as a part, its semicollectivist system, came to an end, and developments started which brought the question of the courage to be as oneself to the fore.

Neocollectivist Manifestations of the Courage to Be as a Part

In reaction to the predominance of the courage to be as oneself in modern Western history, movements of a neocollectivist character have arisen: fascism, nazism, and communism. The basic difference of all of them from primitive collectivism and medieval semicollectivism is threefold. First, neocollectivism is preceded by the liberation of autonomous reason and the creation of a technical civilization. It uses the scientific and technical achievements of this development for its purposes. Secondly, neocollectivism has arisen in a situation where it meets many competing tendencies, even within the neocollectivist movement. Therefore it is less stable and safe than the older forms of collectivism. This leads to the third and most conspicuous difference: the totalitarian methods of present collectivism in terms of a national state or a supranational empire. The reason for this is the necessity for a centralized technical organization and even more for the suppression of tendencies which could dissolve the collectivist system by alternatives and individual decisions. But these three differences do not prevent neocollectivism from showing many traits of the primitive collectivisms, above all the exclusive emphasis on self-affirmation by participation, on the courage to be as a part.

The relapse to tribal collectivism was readily visible in Nazism. The German idea of the *Volksgeist* (national spirit) was a good basis for it. The "blood and soil" mythology strengthened this tendency, and the mystical deification of the Führer did the rest. In comparison with it, original communism was rational eschatology, a movement of criticism and expectation, in many respects similar to the prophetic ideas. However, after the establishment of the Communist state in Russia, the rational and eschatological elements were thrown out and disappeared, and the relapse to tribal collectivism was pushed in all spheres of life. Russian nationalism in its political and in its mystical expressions was amalgamated with the Communist ideology. Today "cosmopolitan" is the name for the worst heretic in the Communist countries. The Communists in spite of their prophetic background, their valuation of reason, and their tremendous technical productivity have almost reached the stage of tribal collectivism.

Therefore it is possible to analyze the courage to be as a part in neocollectivism by looking mainly at its Communist manifestation. Its world historical significance must be seen in the light of an ontology of self-affirmation and courage. One would avoid the issue if one derived the characteristics of Communist neocollectivism from contributing causes like the Russian character, the history of Tsarism, the terror of Stalinism, the dynamics of a totalitarian system, the world political constellation. All these things contribute but are not the source. They help to preserve and to spread the system but they do not constitute its essence. Its essence is the courage to be as a part which it gives to masses of people who lived under an increasing threat of nonbeing and a growing feeling of anxiety. The traditional ways of life from which they got either inherited forms of the courage to be as a part or, since the 19th century, new possibilities of the courage to be as oneself, were rapidly uprooted in the modern world. This has happened and is happening in Europe as well as in the remotest corners of Asia and Africa. It is a world-wide development. And communism gives to those who have lost or are losing their old collectivist self-affirmation a new collectivism and with it a new courage to be as a part. If we look at the convinced adherents of communism we find the willingness to sacrifice any individual fulfillment to the self-affirmation of the group and to the goal of the movement. But perhaps the Communist fighter would not approve of such a description of what he does. Perhaps, like fanatical believers in all movements, he would not feel that he makes a sacrifice. He may feel that he has taken the only right way in which to reach his own fulfillment. If he affirms himself by affirming the collective in which he participates, he receives himself back from the collective, filled and fulfilled by it. He gives much of what belongs to his individual self, perhaps its existence as a particular being in time and space, but he receives more because his true being is enclosed in the being of the group. In surrendering himself to the cause of the collective he surrenders that in him which is not included in the self-affirmation of the collective; and this he does not deem to be worthy of affirmation. In this way the anxiety of individual nonbeing is transformed into anxiety about the collective, and anxiety about the collective is conquered by the courage to affirm oneself through participation in the collective.

This can be shown in relation to the three main types of anxiety. As in every human being the anxiety of fate and death is present in the convinced Communist. No being can accept its own nonbeing without a negative reaction. The terror of the totalitarian state would be meaningless without the possibility of producing terror in its subjects. But the anxiety of fate and death is taken into the courage to be as a part within the whole by whose terror one is threatened. Through the participation one affirms that which may become a destructive fate or even the cause of death for oneself. A more penetrating analysis shows the following structure: Participation is partial identity, partial nonidentity. Fate and death may hurt or destroy that part of oneself that is not identical with the collective in which one participates. But there is another part according to the partial identity of participation. And this other part is neither hurt nor destroyed by the demands and actions of the whole. It transcends fate and death. It is eternal in the sense in which the collective is considered to be eternal, namely as an essential manifestation of being universal. All this need not be conscious in the members of the collective. But it is implicit in their emotions and actions. They are infinitely concerned about the fulfillment of the group. And from this concern they derive their courage to be. The term eternal should not be confused with immortal. There is no idea of individual immortality in old and new collectivism. The collective in which one participates replaces individual immortality. On the other hand, it is not a resignation to annihilation—otherwise no courage to be would be possible —but it is something above both immortality and annihilation; it is the participation in something which transcends death, namely the collective, and through it, in being-itself. He who is in this position feels in the moment of the sacrifice of his life that he is taken into the life of the collective and through it into the life of the universe as an integral element of it, even if not as a particular being. This is similar to the Stoic courage to be; and it is in the last analysis Stoicism that underlies this attitude. It is true today as it was in later antiquity that the Stoic attitude, even if appearing in a collectivist form, is the only serious alternative to Christianity. The difference between the genuine Stoic and the neocollectivist is that the latter is bound in the first place to the collective and in the second place to the universe, while the Stoic was first of all related to the universal Logos and secondly to possible human groups. But in both cases the anxiety of fate and death is taken into the courage to be as a part.

In the same way the anxiety of doubt and meaninglessness is taken into neocollectivist courage. The strength of the Communist self-affirmation prevents the actualization of doubt and the outbreak of the anxiety of meaninglessness. The meaning of life is the meaning of the collective. Even those who live as victims of the terror at the lowest level of the social hierarchy do not doubt the validity of the principles. What happens to them is a problem of fate and demands the courage to overcome the anxiety of fate and death and not the anxiety of doubt and meaninglessness. In this certainty the Communist looks contemptuously at Western society. He observes the large amount of anxiety of doubt in it, and he interprets this as the main symptom of the morbidity and approaching end of bourgeois society. This is one of the reasons for the expulsion and prohibition of most of the modern forms of artistic expression in the neocollectivist countries, although they have made important contributions to the rise and development of modern art and literature in their last pre-Communist period, and although communism, in its fighting stage, has used their antibourgeois elements for its propaganda. With the establishment of the collective and the exclusive emphasis on self-affirmation as a part, those expressions of the courage to be as oneself had to be rejected.

The neocollectivist is also able to take the anxiety of guilt and condemnation into his courage to be as a part. It is not his personal sin that produces anxiety of guilt but a real or possible sin against the collective. The collective, in this respect, replaces for him the God of judgment, repentance, punishment, and forgiveness. To the collective he confesses, often in forms reminiscent of early Christianity or later sectarian groups. From the collective he accepts judgment and punishment. To it he directs his desire for forgiveness and his promise of self-transformation. If he is accepted back by it, his guilt is overcome and a new courage to be is possible. These most striking features in the Communist way of life can hardly be understood if one does not go down to their ontological roots and their existential power in a system which is based on the courage to be as a part.

This description is a typological one, as the descriptions of the earlier forms of collectivism were. A typological description presupposes by its very nature that the type is rarely fully actualized. There are degrees of approximation, mixtures, transitions, and deviations. But it was not my intention to give a picture of the Russian situation as a whole, including the significance of the Greek Orthodox Church, or of the different national movements or of individual dissenters. I wanted to describe the neo-collectivist structure and its type of courage, as actualized predominantly in present-day Russia.

THE COURAGE TO BE AS A PART IN DEMOCRATIC CONFORMISM

The same methodological approach is made to what I shall call democratic conformism. Its most characteristic actualization has taken place in present-day America, but its roots go far back into the European past. Like the neo-collectivist way of life it cannot be understood in the light of merely contributing factors as a frontier situation, the need to amalgamate many nationalities, the long isolation from active world politics, the influence of puritanism and so on. In order to understand it one must ask: Which is the type of courage underlying democratic conformism, how does it deal with the anxieties in human existence, and how is it related to neocollectivist self-affirmation on the one hand, to the manifestations of the courage to be as oneself on the other hand? Another remark must be made at the outset. Present-day America has received, since the early 1930's, influences from Europe and Asia which represent either extreme forms of the courage to be as oneself, like Existentialist literature and art, or attempts to overcome the anxiety of our period by different forms of transcendent courage. But these influences are still limited to the intelligentsia and to people whose eyes have been opened by the impact of world historical events to the questions asked by recent Existentialism. They have not reached the masses of people in any social group and they have not changed the basic trends of feeling and thought and the corresponding attitudes and institutions. On the contrary, the trends toward being as a part and toward affirming one's being by participation in given structures of life are rapidly increasing. Conformity is growing, but it has not yet become collectivism.

The Neo-Stoics of the Renaissance, by transforming the courage to accept fate passively (as in the old Stoics) into an active wrestling with fate, actually prepared the way for the courage to be in the democratic conformism of America. In the symbolism of Renaissance art fate is sometimes represented as the wind blowing on the sails of a vessel, while man stands at the steering wheel and determines the direction as much as it can be determined under the given conditions. Man tries to actualize all his potentialities; and his potentialities are inexhaustible. For he is the microcosm, in whom all cosmic forces are potentially present, and who participates in all spheres and strata of the universe. Through him the universe continues the creative process which first has produced him as the aim and the center of the creation. Now man has to shape his world and himself, according to the productive powers given to him. In him nature comes to its fulfillment, it is taken into his knowledge and his transforming technical activity. In the visual arts nature is drawn into the human sphere and man is posited in nature, and both are shown in their ultimate possibilities of beauty.

The bearer of this creative process is the individual who, as an individual, is a unique representative of the universe. Most important is the creative individual, the genius, in whom, as Kant later formulated it, the unconscious creativity of nature breaks into the consciousness of man. Men like Pico della Mirandola, Leonardo da Vinci, Giordano Bruno, Shaftesbury, Goethe, Schelling were inspired by this idea of a participation in the creative process of the universe. In these men enthusiasm and rationality were united. Their courage was both the courage to be as oneself and the courage to be as a part. The doctrine of the individual as the microcosmic participant in the creative process of the macrocosm presented them with the possibility of this synthesis.

Man's productivity moves from potentiality to actuality in such a way that everything actualized has potentialities for further actualization. This is the basic structure of progress. Although described in Aristotelian terminology, the belief in progress is completely different from the attitude of Aristotle and the whole ancient world. In Aristotle the movement from potentiality to actuality is vertical, going from the lower to the higher forms of being. In modern progressivism the movement from potentiality to actuality is horizontal, temporal, futuristic. And this is the main form in which the self-affirmation of modern Western humanity manifested itself. It was courage, for it had to take into itself an anxiety which grew with the growing knowledge of the universe and our world within it. The earth had been thrown out of the center of the world by Copernicus and Galileo. It had become small, and in spite of the "heroic affect" with which Giordano Bruno dived into the infinity of the universe a feeling of being lost in the ocean of cosmic bodies and among the unbreakable rules of their motion crept into the hearts of many. The courage of the modern period was not a simple optimism. It had to take into itself the deep anxiety of nonbeing in a universe without limits and without a humanly understandable meaning. This anxiety could be taken into the courage but it could not be removed, and it came to the surface any time when the courage was weakened.

This is the decisive source of the courage to be as a part in the creative process of nature and history, as it developed in Western civilization and, most conspicuously, in the new world. But it underwent many changes before it turned into the conformistic type of the courage to be as a part which characterizes present-day American democracy. The cosmic enthusiasm of the Renaissance vanished under the influence of Protestantism and rationalism, and when it reappeared in the classic-romantic movements of the late 18th and early 19th centuries it was not able to gain much influence in industrial society. The synthesis between individuality and participation, based on the cosmic enthusiasm, was dissolved. A permanent tension developed between the courage to be as oneself as it was implied in Renaissance individualism and the courage to be as a part as it was implied in Renaissance universalism. Extreme forms of liberalism were challenged by reactionary attempts to re-establish a medieval collectivism or by utopian attempts to produce a new organic society. Liberalism and democracy could clash in two ways: liberalism could undermine the democratic control of society or democracy could become tyrannical and a transition to totalitarian collectivism. Besides these dynamic and violent movements a more static and unaggressive development could take place: the rise of a democratic conformity which restrains all extreme forms of the courage to be as oneself without destroying the liberal elements that distinguish it from collectivism. This was, above all, the way of Great Britain. The tension between liberalism and democracy also explains many traits of American democratic conformism. But behind all these changes remained one thing, the courage to be as a part in the productive process of history. And this is what makes of present-day American courage one of the great types of the courage to be as a part. Its self-affirmation is the affirmation of oneself as a participant in the creative development of mankind.

There is something astonishing in the American courage for an observer who comes from Europe: although mostly symbolized in the early pioneers it is present today in the large majority of people. A person may have experienced a tragedy, a destructive fate, the breakdown of convictions, even guilt and momentary despair: he feels neither destroyed nor meaningless nor condemned nor without hope. When the Roman Stoic experienced the same catastrophes he took them with the courage of resignation. The typical American, after he has lost the foundations of his existence, works for new foundations. This is true of the individual and it is true of the nation as a whole. One can make experiments because an experimental failure does not mean discouragement. The productive process in which one is a participant naturally includes risks, failures, catastrophes. But they do not undermine courage.

This means that it is the productive act itself in which the power and the significance of being is present. This is a partial answer to a question often asked by foreign observers, especially if they are theologians: the question For what? What is the end of all the magnificent means provided by the productive activity of American society? Have not the means swallowed the ends, and does not the unrestricted production of means indicate the absence of ends? Even many born Americans are today inclined to answer the last question affirmatively. But there is more involved in the production of means. It is not the tools and gadgets that are the *telos*, the inner aim of production; it is the production itself. The means are more than means; they are felt as creations, as symbols of the infinite possibilities implied in man's productivity. Being-itself is essentially productive. The way in which the originally religious word "creative" is applied without hesitation by Christian, and non-Christian, alike to man's productive activities indicates that the creative process of history is felt as divine. As such it includes the courage to be as a part of it. (It has seemed to me more adequate to speak in this context of the productive than of the creative process, since the emphasis lies on technical production.)

Originally the democratic-conformist type of the courage to be as a part was in an outspoken way tied up with the idea of progress. The courage to be as a part in the progress of the group to which one belongs, of this nation, of all mankind, is expressed in all specifically American philosophies: pragmatism, process philosophy, the ethics of growth, progressive education, crusading democracy. But this type of courage is not necessarily destroyed if the belief in progress is shaken, as it is today. Progress can mean two things. In every action in which something is produced beyond what was already given, a progress is made (pro-gress means going forward). In this sense action and the belief in progress are inseparable. The other meaning of progress is a universal, metaphysical law of progressive evolution, in which accumulation produces higher and higher forms and values. The existence of such a law cannot be proved. Most processes show that gain and loss are balanced. Nevertheless the new gain is necessary, because otherwise all past gains would also be lost. The courage of participation in the productive process is not dependent on the metaphysical idea of progress.

The courage to be as a part in the productive process takes anxiety in its three main forms into itself. The way in which it deals with the anxiety about fate has been described. This is especially remarkable in a highly competitive society in which the security of the individual is reduced to almost nothing. The anxiety conquered in the courage to be as a part in the productive process is considerable, because the threat of being excluded from such a participation by unemployment or the loss of an economic basis is what, above all, fate means today. Only in the light of this situation can the tremendous impact of the great crisis of the 1930's on the American people, and the frequent loss of the courage to be in it, be understood. The anxiety about death is met in two ways. The reality of death is excluded from daily life to the highest possible degree. The dead are not allowed to show that they are dead; they are transformed into a mask of the living. The other and more important way of dealing with death is the belief in a continuation of life after death, called the immortality of the soul. This is not a Christian and hardly a Platonic doctrine. Christianity speaks of resurrection and eternal life, Platonism of a participation of the soul in the transtemporal sphere of essences. But the modern idea of immortality means a continuous participation in the productive process—"time and world without end." It is not the eternal rest of the individual in God but his unlimited contribution to the dynamics of the universe that gives him the courage to face death. In this kind of hope God is almost unnecessary. He may be considered as the guarantee of immortality, but if not, the belief in immortality is not necessarily shaken. For the courage to be as a part of the productive process, immortality is decisive and not God, except that God is understood as the productive process itself as with some theologians.

The anxiety of doubt and meaninglessness is potentially as great as the anxiety of fate and death. It is rooted in the nature of finite productivity. Although, as we have seen, the tool as a tool is not important but rather the tool as a result of human productivity, the question: for what? cannot be suppressed completely. It is silenced but always ready to come into the open. Today we are witnessing a rise of this anxiety and a weakening of the courage to take it into itself. The anxiety of guilt and condemnation is deeply rooted in the American mind, first through the influence of puritanism, then through the impact of the evangelical-pietistic movements. It is strong even if its religious foundation is undermined. But in connection with the predominance of the courage to be as a part in the productive process it has changed its character. Guilt is produced by manifest shortcomings in adjustments to and achievements within the creative activities of society. It is the social group in which one participates productively that judges, forgives, and restores, after the adjustments have been made and the achievements have become visible. This is the reason for the existential insignificance of the experience of justification or forgiveness of sins in comparison with the striving for sanctification and the transformation of one's own being as well as one's world. A new beginning is demanded and attempted. This is the way in which the courage to be as a part of the productive process takes the anxiety of guilt into itself.

Participation in the productive process demands conformity and adjustment to the ways of social production. This necessity became stronger the more uniform and comprehensive the methods of production became. Technical society grew into fixed patterns. Conformity in those matters which conserve the smooth functioning of the big machine of production and consumption increased with the increasing impact of the means of public communication. World political thinking, the struggle with collectivism, forced collectivist features on those who fought against them. This process is still going on and may lead to a strengthening of the conformist elements in the type of the courage to be as a part which is represented by America. Conformism might approximate collectivism, not so much in economic respects, and not too much in political respects, but very much in the pattern of daily life and thought. Whether this will happen or not, and if it does to what degree, is partly dependent on the power of resistance in those who represent the opposite pole of the courage to be, the courage to be as oneself. Since their criticism of the conformist and collectivist forms of the courage to be as a part is a decisive element of their self-expression, it will be discussed in the next chapter. The one point, however, in which all criticisms agree is the threat to the individual self in the several forms of the courage to be as a part. It is the danger of loss of self which elicits the protest against them and gives rise to the courage to be as oneself—a courage which itself is threatened by the loss of the world.

THE RISE OF MODERN INDIVIDUALISM
AND THE COURAGE TO BE AS ONESELF

Individualism is the self-affirmation of the individual self as individual self without regard to its participation in its world. As such it is the opposite of collectivism, the self-affirmation of the self as part of a larger whole without regard to its character as an individual self. Individualism has developed out of the bondage of primitive collectivism and medieval semicollectivism. It could grow under the protective cover of democratic conformity, and it has come into the open in moderate or radical forms within the Existentialist movement.

Primitive collectivism was undermined by the experience of personal guilt and individual question-asking. Both were effective at the end of the ancient world and led to the radical nonconformism of the cynics and skeptics, to the moderate nonconformism of the Stoics, and to the attempt to reach a transcendent foundation for the courage to be in Stoicism, mysticism, and Christianity. All these motives were present in medieval semicollectivism, which came to an end like early collectivism with the experience of personal guilt and the analytic power of radical question-asking. But it did not immediately lead to individualism. Protestantism, in spite of its emphasis on the individual conscience, was established as a strictly authoritarian and conformist system, similar to that of its adversary, the Roman Church of the Counter-reformation. There was no individualism in either of the great confessional groups. And there was only hidden individualism outside them, since they had drawn the individualistic trends of the Renaissance into themselves and adapted them to their ecclesiastical conformity.

This situation lasted for 150 years but no more. After this period, that of confessional orthodoxy, the personal element came again to the fore. Pietism and methodism re-emphasized personal guilt, personal experience, and individual perfection. They were not intended to deviate from ecclesiastical conformity, but unavoidably they did deviate; subjective piety became the bridge of the victorious reappearance of autonomous reason. Pietism was the bridge to Enlightenment. But even Enlightenment did not consider itself individualistic. One believed not in a conformity which is based on biblical revelation but in one which should be based on the power of reason in every individual. The principles of practical and theoretical reason were supposed to be universal among men and able to create, with the help of research and education, a new conformity.

The whole period believed in the principle of "harmony"—harmony being the law of the universe according to which the activities of the individual, however individualistically conceived and performed, lead "behind the back" of the single actor to a harmonious whole, to a truth in which at least a large majority can agree, to a good in which more and more people can participate, to a conformity which is based on the free activity of every individual. The individual can be free without destroying the group. The functioning of economic liberalism seemed to confirm this view: the laws of the market produce, behind the backs of the competitors in the market, the greatest possible amount of goods for everybody. The functioning of liberal democracy showed that the freedom of the individual to decide politically does not necessarily destroy political conformity. Scientific progress showed that individual research and the freedom for individual scientific convictions do not prevent a large measure of scientific agreement. Education showed that emphasis on the free development of the individual child does not reduce the chances of his becoming an active member of a conformist society. And the history of Protestantism confirmed the belief of the Reformers that the free encounter of everybody with the Bible can create an ecclesiastical conformity—in spite of individual and even denominational differences. Therefore it was by no means absurd when Leibnitz formulated the law of preestablished harmony by teaching that the monads of which all things consist, although they have no doors and windows that open toward each other, participate in the same world which is present in each of them, whether it be dimly or clearly perceived. The problem of individualization and participation seemed to be solved philosophically as well as practically.

Courage to be as oneself, as this is understood in the Enlightenment, is a courage in which individual self-afirmation includes participation in universal, rational, self-affirmation. Thus it is not the individual self as such which affirms itself but the individual self as the bearer of reason. The courage to be as oneself is the courage to follow reason and to defy irrational authority. In this respect—but only in this respect—it is Neo-Stoicism. For the courage to be of the Enlightenment is not a resigned courage to be. It dares not only to face the vicissitudes of fate and the inescapability of death but to affirm itself as transforming reality according to the demands of reason. It is a fighting, daring courage. It conquers the threat of meaninglessness by courageous action. It conquers the threat of guilt by accepting errors, shortcomings, misdeeds in the individual as well as in social life as unavoidable and at the same time to be overcome by education. The courage to be as oneself within the atmosphere of Enlightenment is the courage to affirm oneself as a bridge from a lower to a higher state of rationality. It is obvious that this kind of courage to be must become conformist the moment its revolutionary attack on that which contradicts reason has ceased, namely in the victorious bourgeoisie.

THE ROMANTIC AND NATURALISTIC FORMS OF THE COURAGE TO BE AS ONESELF

The romantic movement has produced a concept of individuality which is equally to be distinguished from the medieval concept and from that of the Enlightenment and contains elements of both. The individual is emphasized in his uniqueness, as an incomparable and infinitely significant expression of the substance of being. Not conformity but differentiation is the end of the ways of God. Self-affirmation of one's uniqueness and acceptance of the demands of one's individual nature are the right courage to be. This does not necessarily mean willfulness and irrationality, because the uniqueness of one's individuality lies in its creative possibilities. But the danger is obvious. The romantic irony elevated the individual beyond all content and made him empty: he was no longer obliged to participate in anything seriously. In a man like Friedrich von Schlegel the courage to be as an individual self produced complete neglect of participation, but it also produced, in reaction to the emptiness of this self-affirmation, the desire to return to a collective. Schlegel, and with him many extreme individualists in the last hundred years, became Roman Catholics. The courage to be as oneself broke down, and one turned to an institutional embodiment of the courage to be as a part. Such a turn was prepared by the other side of romantic thought, the emphasis on the collectives and semicollectives of the past, the ideal of the "organic society." Organism, as has so often happened in the past, became the symbol of a balance between individualization and participation. However, its historical function in the early 19th century was to express not the need for a balance but the longing for the collectivist pole. It was used by all reactionary groups of this period who, be it for political or for spiritual reasons or both, tried to re-establish a "new Middle Ages." In this way the romantic movement produced both a radical form of the courage to be as oneself and the (unfulfilled) desire for a radical form of the courage to be as a part. Romanticism as an attitude has outlived the romantic movement. So-called Bohemianism was a continuation of the romantic courage to be as oneself. Bohemianism continued the romantic attack on the established bourgeoisie and its conformism. Both the romantic movement and its Bohemian continuation have decisively contributed to present-day Existentialism.

But Bohemianism and Existentialism have received elements of another movement in which the courage to be as oneself was pronounced: naturalism. The word naturalism is used in many different ways. For our purpose it suffices to deal with that type of naturalism in which the individualistic form of the courage to be as oneself is effective. Nietzsche is an outstanding representative of such a naturalism. He is a romantic naturalist and, at the same time, one of the most important—perhaps *the* most important—forerunner of the Existentialist courage to be as oneself. The phrase "romantic naturalist" seems to be a contradiction in terms. The self-transcendence of romantic imagination and the naturalistic self-restriction to the empirically given appear to be separated by a deep gap. But naturalism means the identification of being with nature and the consequent rejection of the supernatural. This definition leaves the question of the nature of the natural wide open. Nature can be described mechanistically. It can be described organologically. It can be described in terms of a necessary progressive integration or of creative evolution. It can be described as a system of laws or of structures or as a mixture of both. Naturalism can take its pattern from the absolutely concrete, the individual self as we find it in man, or from the absolutely abstract, the mathematic equations which determine the character of power fields. All this and much more can be naturalism.

But not all of these types of naturalism are expressions of courage to be as oneself. Only if the individualistic pole in the structure of the natural is decisive can naturalism be romantic and amalgamate with Bohemianism and Existentialism. This is the case in the voluntaristic types of naturalism. If nature (and for naturalism this means "being") is seen as the creative expression of an unconscious will or as the objectivation of the will to power or as the product of the *élan vital*, then the centers of will, the individual selves, are decisive for the movement of the whole. In individuals' self-affirmation life affirms itself or negates itself. Even if the selves are subject to an ultimate cosmic destiny they determine their own being in freedom. A large section of American pragmatism belongs to this group. In spite of American conformism and its courage to be as a part, pragmatism shared many concepts with that perspective more widely known in Europe as the "philosophy of life." Its ethical principle is growth, its educational method is self-affirmation of the individual self, its preferred concept is creativity. The pragmatist philosophers are not always aware of the fact that courage to create implies the courage to replace the old by the new—the new for which there are no norms and criteria, the new which is a risk and which, measured by the old, is incalculable. Their social conformity hides from them what in Europe was expressed openly and consciously. They do not realize that pragmatism in its logical consequence (if not restricted by Christian or humanistic conformity) leads to that courage to be as oneself which is proclaimed by the radical Existentialists. The pragmatist type of naturalism is in its character, though not in its intention, a follower of romantic individualism and a predecessor of Existentialist independentism. The nature of the undirected growth is not different from the nature of the will to power and of the élan vital. But the naturalists themselves are different. The European naturalists are consistent and self-destructive; the American naturalists are saved by a happy inconsistency: they still accept the conformist courage to be as a part.

The courage to be as oneself in all these groups has the character of the self-affirmation of the individual self as individual self in spite of the elements of nonbeing threatening it. The anxiety of fate is conquered by the self-affirmation of the individual as an infinitely significant microcosmic representation of the universe. He mediates the powers of being which are concentrated in him. He has them within himself in knowledge and he transforms them in action. He directs the course of his life, and he can stand tragedy and death in a "heroic affect" and a love for the universe which he mirrors. Even loneliness is not absolute loneliness because the contents of the universe are in him. If we compare this kind of courage with that of the Stoics we find that the main point of difference is in the emphasis on the uniqueness of the individual self in the line of thought which starts in the Renaissance and runs over the romantics to the present. In Stoicism it is the wisdom of the wise man which is essentially equal in everyone out of which his courage to be arises. In the modern world it is the individual as individual. Behind this change lies the Christian valuation of the individual soul as eternally significant. But it is not this doctrine which gives the courage to be to modern man but the doctrine of the individual in his quality as mirror of the universe.

Enthusiasm for the universe, in knowing as well as in creating, also answers the question of doubt and meaninglessness. Doubt is the necessary tool of knowledge. And meaninglessness is no threat so long as enthusiasm for the universe and for man as its center is alive. The anxiety of guilt is removed: the symbols of death, judgment, and hell are put aside. Everything is done to deprive them of their seriousness. The courage of self-affirmation will not be shaken by the anxiety of guilt and condemnation.

In later romanticism another dimension of the anxiety of guilt and its conquest was opened up. The destructive trends in the human soul were discovered. The second period of the romantic movement, in philosophy as well as in poetry, broke away from the ideas of harmony which were decisive from the Renaissance to the classicists and early romantics. In this period, which is represented in philosophy by Schelling and by Schopenhauer, in literature by men like E. T. A. Hoffman, a kind of demonic realism was born, which was tremendously influential on Existentialism and depth psychology. The courage to affirm oneself must include the courage to affirm one's own demonic depth. This contradicted radically the moral conformism of the average Protestant and even of the average humanist. But it was avidly accepted by the Bohemian and the romantic naturalists. The courage to take the anxiety of the demonic upon oneself in spite of its destructive and often despairing character was the form in which the anxiety of guilt was conquered. But this was possible only because the personal quality of evil had been removed by the preceding development and could now be replaced by the cosmic evil, which is structural and not a matter of personal responsibility. The courage to take the anxiety of guilt upon oneself has become the courage to affirm the demonic trends within oneself. This could happen because the demonic was not considered unambiguously negative but was thought to be part of the creative power of being. The demonic as the ambiguous ground of the creative is a discovery of the later period of romanticism, which over the bridges of Bohemianism and naturalism was brought to the Existentialism of the 20th century. Its confirmation in scientific terms was depth psychology.

In some respects all these forms of the individualistic courage to be are forerunners of the radicalism of the 20th century, in which the courage to be as oneself was brought to most powerful expression in the Existentialist movement. The survey given in this chapter shows that the courage to be as oneself is never completely separated from the other pole, the courage to be as a part; and even more, that overcoming isolation and facing the danger of losing one's world in the self-affirmation of oneself as an individual are a way toward something which transcends both self and world. Ideas like the microcosm mirroring the universe, or the monad representing the world, or the individual will to power expressing the character of will to power in life itself—all these point to a solution which transcends the two types of the courage to be.

EXISTENTIALIST FORMS OF THE COURAGE TO BE AS ONESELF

THE EXISTENTIAL ATTITUDE AND EXISTENTIALISM

Late romanticism, Bohemianism, and romantic naturalism have prepared the way for present-day Existentialism, the most radical form of the courage to be as oneself. In spite of the large amount of literature which has appeared recently about Existentialism it is necessary for our purpose to deal with it from the point of view of its ontological character and its relation to the courage to be.

We must first of all distinguish the existential attitude from philosophical or artistic Existentialism. The existential attitude is one of involvement in contrast to a merely theoretical or detached attitude. "Existential" in this

sense can be defined as participating in a situation, especially a cognitive situation, with the whole of one's existence. This includes temporal, spatial, historical, psychological, sociological, biological conditions. And it includes the finite freedom which reacts to these con ˙
changes them. An existential knowledge is a knowledge in which these elements, and therefore the whole existence of him who knows, participate. This seems to contradict the necessary objectivity of the cognitive act and the demand for detachment in it. But knowledge depends on its object. There are realms of reality or—more exactly—of abstraction from reality in which the most complete detachment is the adequate cognitive approach. Everything which can be expressed in terms of quantitative measurement has this character. But it is most inadequate to apply the same approach to reality in its infinite concreteness. A self which has become a matter of calculation and management has ceased to be a self. It has become a thing. You must participate in a self in order to know what it is. But by participating you change it. In all existential knowledge both subject and object are transformed by the very act of knowing. Existential knowledge is based on an encounter in which a new meaning is created and recognized. The knowledge of another person, the knowledge of history, the knowledge of a spiritual creation, religious knowledge —all have existential character. This does not exclude theoretical objectivity on the basis of detachment. But it restricts detachment to one element within the embracing act of cognitive participation. You may have a precise

detached knowledge of another person, his psychological type and his calculable reactions, but in knowing this you do not know the person, his centered self, his knowledge of himself. Only in participating in his self, in performing an existential break-through into the center of his being, will you know him in the situation of your break-through to him. This is the first meaning of "existential," namely existential as the attitude of participating with one's own existence in some other existence.

The other meaning of "existential" designates a content and not an attitude. It points to a special form of philosophy: to Existentialism. We have to deal with it because it is the expression of the most radical form of the courage to be as oneself. But before going into it we must show why both an attitude and a content are described with words which are derived from the same word, "existence." The existential attitude and the Existentialist content have in common an interpretation of the human situation which conflicts with a nonexistential interpretation. The latter asserts that man is able to transcend, in knowledge and life, the finitude, the estrangement, and the ambiguities of human existence. Hegel's system is the classical expression of essentialism. When Kierkegaard broke away from Hegel's system of essences he did two things: he proclaimed an existential attitude and he instigated a philosophy of existence. He realized that the knowledge of that which concerns us infinitely is possible only in an attitude of infinite concern, in an existential attitude. At the same time he developed a doctrine of man which describes the estrangement of man from his essential nature in terms of anxiety and despair. Man in the existential situation of finitude and estrangement can reach truth only in an existential attitude. "Man does not sit on the throne of God," participating in his essential knowledge of everything that is. Man has no place of pure objectivity above finitude and estrangement. His cognitive function is as existentially conditioned as his whole being. This is the connection of the two meanings of "existential."

THE EXISTENTIALIST POINT OF VIEW

Turning now to Existentialism not as an attitude but as a content, we can distinguish three meanings: Existentialism as a *point of view*, as *protest*, and as *expression*. The Existentialist point of view is present in most theology and in much philosophy, art, and literature. But it remains a point of view, sometimes without being recognized as such. After some isolated forerunners had appeared Existentialism as protest became a conscious movement with the second third of the 19th century, and as such has largely determined the destiny of the 20th century. Existentialism as expression is the character of the philosophy, art, and literature of the period of the World Wars and all-prevading anxiety of doubt and meaninglessness. It is the expression of our own situation.

A few examples of the Existentialist point of view may be given. Most characteristic, and at the same time most decisive for the whole development of all forms of Existentialism, is Plato. Following the Orphic descriptions of

the human predicament he teaches the separation of the
human soul from its "home" in the realm of pure essences.
Man is estranged from what he essentially is. His existence
in a transitory world contradicts his essential participation
in the eternal world of ideas. This is expressed in mythological terms, because existence resists conceptualization.
Only the realm of essences admits of structural analysis.
Wherever Plato uses a myth he describes the transition
from one's essential being to one's existential estrangement, and the return from the latter to the former. The
Platonic distinction between the essential and the existential realms is fundamental for all later developments. It
lies in the background even of present-day Existentialism.

Other examples of the Existentialist point of view are
the classical Christian doctrines of the fall, sin, and salvation. Their structure is analogous to the Platonic distinc-
tions. As in Plato, the essential nature of man and his
world is good. It is good in Christian thought because it
is a divine creation. But man's essential or created goodness has been lost. The fall and sin have corrupted not only
his ethical but also his cognitive qualities. He is subjected
to the conflicts of existence and his reason is not exempted
from them. But as in Plato a transhistorical memory has
never been lost even in the most estranged forms of human
existence, so in Christianity the essential structure of man
and his world is preserved by the sustaining and directing
creativity of God, which makes not only some goodness
but also some truth possible. Only because this is so is man

able to realize the conflicts of his existential predicament and to expect a restitution of his essential status.

Platonism as well as classical Christian theology have the Existentialist point of view. It determines their understanding of the human situation. But neither of them is Existentialist in the technical sense of the term. The Existentialist point of view is effective within the frame of their Essentialist ontology. This is true not only of Plato but also of Augustine, although his theology contains more profound insights into the negativities of the human predicament than that of anyone else in early Christianity, and although he had to defend his doctrine of man against the Essentialist moralism of Pelagius.

Continuing the Augustinian analysis of man's predicament, we note that monastic and mystical self-scrutiny brought to light an immense amount of the material of depth psychology, which entered theology in its chapters on man's creatureliness, sin, and sanctification. It also appeared in the medieval understanding of the demonic, and it was used by the confessors, especially in the monasteries. Much of the material which is discussed today by depth psychology and contemporary Existentialism was not unknown to the religious "analysts" of the Middle Ages. It was still known to the Reformers, notably to Luther, whose dialectical descriptions of the ambiguities of goodness, of demonic despair and of the necessity for Divine forgiveness have deep roots in the medieval search for the human soul in its relation to God.

The greatest poetic expression of the Existentialist point

of view in the Middle Ages is Dante's *Divina Comedia*. It remains, like the religious depth psychology of the monastics, within the framework of scholastic ontology. But within these limits it enters the deepest places of human self-destruction and despair as well as the highest places of courage and salvation, and gives in poetic symbols an all-embracing existential doctrine of man. Some Renaissance artists have anticipated recent Existentialist art in their drawings and paintings. The demonic subjects to which were attracted men like Bosch, Breughel, Grünewald, the Spaniards and south Italians, the late Gothic masters of mass scenes, and many others are expressions of an Existentialist understanding of the human situation (see for example Breughel's Tower of Babel pictures). But in none of them was the medieval tradition completely broken. It was still an Existentialist point of view and not yet Existentialism.

In connection with the rise of modern individualism I have mentioned the nominalistic splitting of universals into individual things. There is a side in nominalism which anticipates motifs of recent Existentialism. This is, for example, its irrationalism, rooted in the breakdown of the philosophy of essences under the attacks of Duns Scotus and Ockham. The emphasis on the contingency of everything that exists makes both the will of God and the being of man equally contingent. It gives to man the feeling of a definite lack of ultimate necessity, with respect not only to himself but also to his world. And it gives him a corresponding anxiety. Another motif of recent Existentialism anticipated by nominalism is the escape into authority, which is a consequence of the dissolution of universals and the inability of the isolated individual to develop the courage to be as oneself. Therefore the nominalists built the bridge to an ecclesiastical authoritarianism which surpassed everything in the early and later Middle Ages and produced modern Catholic collectivism. But even so, nominalism was not Existentialism, although it was one of the most important forerunners of the Existentialist courage to be as oneself. It did not take this step, because even nominalism did not intend to break away from the medieval tradition.

What is the courage to be, in a situation where the Existentialist point of view has not yet burst the Essentialist frame? Generally speaking, it is the courage to be as a part. But this answer is not sufficient. Where there is an Existentialist point of view there is the problem of the human situation experienced by the individual. In the conclusion of the *Gorgias* Plato brings the individuals before the judge of the underworld, Rhadamanthus, who decides on their personal righteousness or injustice. In classical Christianity the eternal judgment concerns the individual; in Augustine the universality of original sin does not change the dualism in the eternal destiny of the individual; monastic and mystical self-scrutiny concerns the individual self; Dante puts the individual, according to his special character, into the different sections of reality; the painters of the demonic produce the feeling that the individual is lonely in the world as it is; nominalism isolates the individual consciously. Nevertheless, the courage to be in all these cases is not the courage to be as oneself. In each case it is an embracing whole from which the courage to be is derived: the heavenly realm, the Kingdom of God, divine grace, the providential structure of reality, the authority of the Church. Yet it is not a return to the unbroken courage to be as a part. It is much more a going ahead or above to a source of courage which transcends both the courage to be a part and the courage to be as oneself.

THE LOSS OF THE EXISTENTIALIST
POINT OF VIEW

The Existentialist revolt of the 19th century is a reaction against the loss of the Existentialist point of view since the beginning of modern times. While the first part of the Renaissance as represented by Nicholas of Cusa, the academy of Florence, and early Renaissance painting was still determined by the Augustinian tradition, the later Renaissance broke away from it and created a new scientific essentialism. In Descartes the anti-Existential bias is most conspicuous. The existence of man and his world is put into "brackets"—as Husserl, who derives his "phenomenological" method from Descartes, has formulated it. Man becomes pure consciousness, a naked epistemological subject; the world (including man's psychosomatic being) becomes an object of scientific inquiry and technical management. Man in his existential predicament disappears. It was, therefore, quite adequate when recent

philosophical Existentialism showed that behind the *sum*
(I am) in Descartes' *Cogito ergo sum* lies the problem of
the nature of this *sum* which is more than mere *cogitatio*
(consciousness)—namely existence in time and space and
under the conditions of finitude and estrangement.

Protestantism in its rejection of ontology seemed to
re-emphasize the Existentialist point of view. And indeed
the Protestant reduction of the dogma to the confrontation of human sin and divine forgiveness, and the presup-
positions and implications of this confrontation, served
the Existentialist point of view—but with a decisive limitation: the abundance of Existentialist material discovered
in connection with the monastic self-scrutiny of the Middle Ages was lost, not in the Reformers themselves but in
their followers, whose emphasis was on the doctrines of
justification and predestination. The Protestant theologians stressed the unconditional character of the divine
judgment and the free character of God's forgiveness.
They were suspicious of an analysis of human existence,
they were not interested in the relativities and ambiguities
of the human condition. On the contrary: they believed
that such considerations would weaken the absolute No
and Yes which characterizes the divine-human relationship. But the consequence of this nonexistential teaching
of the Protestant theologians was that the doctrinal concepts of the biblical message were preached as objective
truth without any attempt to mediate the message to man
in his psychosomatic and psychosocial existence. (It was
only under pressure of the social movements of the late

19th century and the psychological movements of the 20th century that Protestantism became more open to the existential problems of the contemporary situation.) In Calvinism and sectarianism man became more and more transformed into an abstract moral subject, as in Descartes he was considered an epistemological subject. And when in the 18th century the content of Protestant ethics became adjusted to the demands of the rising industrial society which called for a reasonable management of oneself and one's world, anti-Existentialist philosophy and anti-Existentialist theology merged. The rational subject, moral and scientific, replaced the existential subject, his conflicts and despairs.

One of the leaders of this development, the teacher of ethical autonomy, Immanuel Kant, reserved two places in his philosophy for the Existentialist point of view, one in his doctrine of the distance between finite man and ultimate reality and the other in his doctrine of the perversion of man's rationality by radical evil. But for these Existentialist notions he was attacked by many of his admirers, including the greatest of them, Goethe and Hegel. Both these critics were predominantly anti-Existentialist. In Hegel's attempt to interpret all reality in terms of a system of essences whose more or less adequate expression is the existing world the Essentialist trend of modern philosophy reached its climax. Existence was resolved into essence. The world is reasonable as it is. Existence is a necessary expression of essence. History is the manifestation of essential being under the conditions of existence. Its course can be understood and justified. A courage which conquers the negativities of the individual life is possible for those who participate in the universal process in which the absolute mind actualizes itself. The anxieties of fate, guilt, and doubt are overcome by means of an elevation through the different degrees of meanings toward the highest, the philosophical intuition of the universal process itself. Hegel tries to unite the courage to be as a part (especially of a nation) with the courage to be as oneself (especially as a thinker) in a courage which transcends both and has a mystical background.

It is, however, misleading to neglect the Existentialist elements in Hegel. They are much stronger than is usually recognized. First of all Hegel is conscious of the ontology of nonbeing. Negation is the dynamic power of his system, driving the absolute idea (the essential realm) toward existence and driving existence back toward the absolute idea (which in the process actualizes itself as the absolute mind or spirit). Hegel knows of the mystery and anxiety of nonbeing; but he takes it into the self-affirmation of being. A second Existentialist element in Hegel is his doctrine that within existence nothing great is achieved without passion and interest. This formula of his introduction to the *Philosophy of History* shows that Hegel was aware of the insights of the romantics and the philosophers of life into the nonrational levels of human nature. The third element, which like the two others deeply influenced Hegel's Existentialist enemies, was the realistic valuation of the predicament of the individual within the process of history. History, he says, in the same introduction, is not a place where the individual can reach happiness. This implies either that the individual must elevate himself above the universal process to the situation of the intuiting philosopher or that the existential problem of the individual is not solved. And this was the basis for the Existentialist protest against Hegel and the world which is mirrored in his philosophy.

EXISTENTIALISM AS REVOLT

The revolt against Hegel's Essentialist philosophy was accomplished with the help of Existentialist elements present, though subdued, in Hegel himself. The first to lead the Existentialist attack was Hegel's former friend Schelling, on whom Hegel had been dependent in earlier years. In his old age Schelling presented his so-called "Positive Philosophie," most of the concepts of which were used by the revolutionary Existentialists of the 19th century. He called Essentialism "negative philosophy" because it abstracts from real existence, and he called Positive Philosophie the thought of the individual who experiences and thinks, and decides within his historical situation. He was the first to use the term "existence" in contradicting philosophical Essentialism. Although his philosophy was rejected because of the Christian myth which he reinterpreted philosophically in Existentialist terms, he influenced many people, notably Soren Kierkegaard.

Schopenhauer used the voluntarist tradition for his

anti-Essentialist thinking. He rediscovered characteristics of the human soul and of man's existential predicament which had been covered by the Essentialist tendency of modern thought. At the same time Feuerbach emphasized the material conditions of human existence, and derived religious faith from the desire of man to overcome finitude in a transcendent world. Max Stirner wrote a book in which the courage to be as oneself was expressed in terms of a practical solipsism that destroyed any communication between man and man. Marx belonged to the Existentialist revolt, insofar as he contrasted the actual existence of man under the system of early capitalism with Hegel's Essentialist description of man's reconciliation with himself in the present world. Most important of all the Existentialists was Nietzsche, who in his description of European nihilism presented the picture of a world in which human existence has fallen into utter meaninglessness. Philosophers of life and pragmatists tried to derive the split between subject and object from something which precedes both of them—"life"—and to interpret the objectified world as a self-negation of the creative life (Dilthey, Bergson, Simmel, James). One of the greatest scholars of the 19th century, Max Weber, described the tragic self-destruction of life once technical reason has come into control. At the end of the century all this was still protest. The situation itself was not visibly changed.

Since the last decades of the 19th century revolt against the objectified world has determined the character of art and literature. While the great French impressionists, in spite of their emphasis on subjectivity, did not transcend the split between subjectivity and objectivity but treated the subject itself as a scientific object, the situation changed with Cézanne, Van Gogh, and Munch. From this time on, the question of existence appeared in the disturbing forms of artistic expressionism. The Existentialist revolt, in all its phases, produced a tremendous amount of psychological material. Existentialist revolutionaries like Baudelaire and Rimbaud in poetry, Flaubert and Dostoievsky in the novel, Ibsen and Strindberg in the theater are full of discoveries in the deserts and jungles of the human soul. Their insights were confirmed and methodologically organized by depth psychology, which started at the end of the century. When with July 31, 1914, the 19th century came to an end, the Existentialist revolt ceased to be revolt. It became the mirror of an experienced reality.

It was the threat of an infinite loss, namely the loss of their individual persons, which drove the revolutionary Existentialists of the 19th century to their attack. They realized that a process was going on in which people were transformed into things, into pieces of reality which pure science can calculate and technical science can control. The idealistic wing of bourgeois thinking made of the person a vessel in which universals find a more or less adequate place. The naturalistic wing of bourgeois thinking made of the person an empty field into which sense impressions enter and prevail according to the degree of their intensity. In both cases the individual self is an empty space and the bearer of something which is not himself, something strange by which the self is estranged from itself. Idealism and naturalism are alike in their attitude to the existing person; both of them eliminate his infinite significance and make him a space through which something else passes. Both philosophies are expressions of a society which was devised for the liberation of man but which fell under the bondage of objects it itself had created. The safety which is guaranteed by well-functioning mechanisms for the technical control of nature, by the refined psychological control of the person, by the rapidly increasing organizational control of society —this safety is bought at a high price: man, for whom all this was invented as a means, becomes a means himself in the service of means. This is the background of Pascal's attack on the rule of mathematical rationality in the 17th century; it is the background of the romantics' attack on the rule of moral rationality in the late 18th century; it is the background of Kierkegaard's attack on the rule of depersonalizing logic in Hegel's thought. It is the background of Marx's fight against economic dehumanization, of Nietzsche's struggle for creativity, of Bergson's fight against the spatial realm of dead objects. It is the background of the desire of most of the philosophers of life to save life from the destructive power of self-objectivation. They struggled for the preservation of the person, for the self-affirmation of the self, in a situation in which the self was more and more lost in its world. They tried to indicate a way for the courage to be as oneself under conditions which annihilate the self and replace it by the thing.

EXISTENTIALISM TODAY
AND THE COURAGE OF DESPAIR

COURAGE AND DESPAIR

Existentialism as it appeared in the 20th century represents the most vivid and threatening meaning of "existential." In it the whole development comes to a point beyond which it cannot go. It has become a reality in all the countries of the Western world. It is expressed in all the realms of man's spiritual creativity, it penetrates all educated classes. It is not the invention of a Bohemian philosopher or of a neurotic novelist; it is not a sensational exaggeration made for the sake of profit and fame; it is not a morbid play with negativities. Elements of all these have entered it, but it itself is something else. It is the expression of the anxiety of meaninglessness and of the attempt to take this anxiety into the courage to be as oneself.

Recent Existentialism must be considered from these two points of view. It is not simply individualism of the rationalistic or romantic or naturalistic type. In distinction to these three preparatory movements it has experienced the universal breakdown of meaning. Twentieth-century man has lost a meaningful world and a self which lives in meanings out of a spiritual center. The man-created world of objects has drawn into itself him who created it and who now loses his subjectivity in it. He has sacrificed himself to his own productions. But man still is aware of what he has lost or is continuously losing. He is still man enough to experience his dehumanization as despair. He does not know a way out but he tries to save his humanity by expressing the situation as without an "exit." He reacts with the courage of despair, the courage to take his despair upon himself and to resist the radical threat of nonbeing by the courage to be as oneself. Every analyst of present-day Existentialist philosophy, art, and literature can show their ambiguous structure: the meaninglessness which drives to despair, a passionate denunciation of this situation, and the successful or unsuccessful attempt to take the anxiety of meaninglessness into the courage to be as oneself.

It is not astonishing that those who are unshaken in their courage to be as a part, either in its collectivist or in its conformist form, are disturbed by the expressions of the Existentialist courage of despair. They are unable to understand what is happening in our period. They are unable to distinguish the genuine from the neurotic anxiety in Existentialism. They attack as a morbid longing for negativity what in reality is courageous acceptance of the negative. They call decay what is actually the creative expression of decay. They reject as meaningless the meaningful attempt to reveal the meaninglessness of our situation. It is not the ordinary difficulty of understanding those who break new ways in thinking and artistic expression which produces the widespread resistance to recent Existentialism but the desire to protect a self-limiting courage to be as a part. Somehow one feels that this is not a true safety; one has to suppress inclinations to accept the Existentialist visions, one even enjoys them if they appear in the theater or in novels, but one refuses to take them seriously, that is as revelations of one's own existential meaninglessness and hidden despair. The violent reactions against modern art in collectivist (Nazi, Communist) as well as conformist (American democratic) groups show that they feel seriously threatened by it. But one does not feel spiritually threatened by something which is not an element of oneself. And since it is a symptom of the neurotic character to resist nonbeing by reducing being, the Existentialist could reply to the frequent reproach that he is neurotic by showing the neurotic defense mechanisms of the anti-Existentialist desire for traditional safety.

There should be no question of what Christian theology has to do in this situation. It should decide for truth against safety, even if the safety is consecrated and supported by the churches. Certainly there is a Christian conformism, from the beginning of the Church on, and there is a Christian collectivism—or at least semicollectivism, in several periods of Church history. But this should not induce Christian theologians to identify Christian courage with the courage to be as a part. They should realize that the courage to be as oneself is the necessary corrective to the courage to be as a part—even if they rightly assume that neither of these forms of the courage to be gives the final solution.

THE COURAGE OF DESPAIR IN
CONTEMPORARY ART AND LITERATURE

The courage of despair, the experience of meaningless-ness, and the self-affirmation in spite of them are manifest in the Existentialists of the 20th century. Meaninglessness is the problem of all of them. The anxiety of doubt and meaninglessness is, as we have seen, the anxiety of our period. The anxiety of fate and death and the anxiety of guilt and condemnation are implied but they are not de-cisive. When Heidegger speaks about the anticipation of one's own death it is not the question of immortality which concerns him but the question of what the anticipa-tion of death means for the human situation. When Kierkegaard deals with the problem of guilt it is not the theological question of sin and forgiveness that moves him but the question of what the possibility of personal existence is in the light of personal guilt. The problem of meaning troubles recent Existentialists even when they speak of finitude and guilt.

The decisive event which underlies the search for meaning and the despair of it in the 20th century is the loss of God in the 19th century. Feuerbach explained God away in terms of the infinite desire of the human heart; Marx explained him away in terms of an ideological at-tempt to rise above the given reality; Nietzsche as a weak-ening of the will to live. The result is the pronouncement "God is dead," and with him the whole system of values and meanings in which one lived. This is felt both as a loss and as a liberation. It drives one either to nihilism or to the courage which takes nonbeing into itself. There is probably nobody who has influenced modern Existentialism as much as Nietzsche and there is probably nobody who has presented the will to be oneself more consistently and more absurdly. In him the feeling of meaninglessness became despairing and self-destructive.

On this basis Existentialism, that is the great art, literature, and philosophy of the 20th century, reveal the courage to face things as they are and to express the anxiety of meaninglessness. It is creative courage which appears in the creative expressions of despair. Sartre calls one of his most powerful plays *No Exit*, a classical formula for the situation of despair. But he himself has an exit: he can *say* "no exit," thus taking the situation of meaninglessness upon himself. T. S. Eliot called his first great poem "The Wasteland." He described the decomposition of civilization, the lack of conviction and direction, the poverty and hysteria of the modern consciousness (as one of his critics has analyzed it). But it is the beautifully cultivated garden of a great poem which describes the meaninglessness of the Wasteland and expresses the courage of despair.

In Kafka's novels *The Castle* and *The Trial* the unapproachable remoteness of the source of meaning and the obscurity of the source of justice and mercy are expressed in language which is pure and classical. The courage to take upon oneself the loneliness of such creativity and the horror of such visions is an outstanding expression of the courage to be as oneself. Man is separated from the sources of courage—but not completely: he is still able to face and to accept his own separation. In Auden's the *Age of Anxiety* the courage to take upon oneself the anxiety in a world which has lost the meaning is as obvious as the profound experience of this loss: the two poles which are united in the phrase "courage of despair" receive equal emphasis. In Sartre's *The Age of Reason* the hero faces a situation in which his passionate desire to be himself drives him to the rejection of every human commitment. He refuses to accept anything which could limit his freedom. Nothing has ultimate meaning for him, neither love nor friendship nor politics. The only immovable point is the unlimited freedom to change, to preserve freedom without content. He represents one of the most extreme forms of the courage to be as oneself, the courage to be a self which is free from any bond and which pays the price of complete emptiness. In the invention of such a figure Sartre proves his courage of despair. From the opposite side, the same problem is faced in the novel *The Stranger* by Camus, who stands on the boundary line of Existentialism but who sees the problem of meaninglessness as sharply as the Existentialists. His hero is a man without subjectivity. He is not extraordinary in any respect. He acts as any ordinary official in a small position would act. He is a stranger because he nowhere achieves an existential relation to himself or to his world. Whatever happens to him has no reality and meaning to him: a love which is not a real love, a trial which is not a real trial, an execution which has no justification in reality. There is neither guilt nor forgiveness, neither despair nor courage in him. He is described not as a person but as a psychological process which is completely conditioned, whether he works or loves or kills or eats or sleeps. He is an object among objects, without meaning for himself and therefore unable to find meaning in his world. He represents that destiny of absolute objectivation against which all Existentialists fight. He represents it in the most radical way, without reconciliation. The courage to create this figure equals the courage with which Kafka has created the figure of Mr. K.

A glimpse at the theater confirms this picture. The theater, especially in the United States, is full of images of meaninglessness and despair. In some plays nothing else is shown (as in Arthur Miller's *Death of a Salesman*); in others the negativity is less unconditional (as in Tennessee Williams' *A Streetcar Named Desire*). But it seldom becomes positivity: even comparatively positive solutions are undermined by doubt and by awareness of the ambiguity of all solutions. It is astonishing that these plays are attended by large crowds in a country whose prevailing courage is the courage to be as a part in a system of democratic conformity. What does this mean for the situation of America and with it of mankind as a whole? One can easily play down the importance of this phenomenon. One can point to the unquestionable fact that even the largest crowds of theatergoers are an infinitely small percentage of the American population. One can dismiss the significance of the attraction the Existentialist theater has for many by calling it an imported fashion, doomed to disappear very soon. This is possibly but not necessarily so. It may be that the comparatively few (few even if one adds to them all the cynics and despairing ones in our institutions of higher learning) are a vanguard which precedes a great change in the spiritual and social-psychological situation. It may be that the limits of the courage to be as a part have become visible to more people than the increasing conformity shows. If this is the meaning of the appeal that Existentialism has on the stage, one should observe it carefully and prevent it from becoming the forerunner of collectivist forms of the courage to be as a part—a threat which history has abundantly proved to exist.

The combination of the experience of meaninglessness and of the courage to be as oneself is the key to the development of visual art since the turn of the century. In expressionism and surrealism the surface structures of reality are disrupted. The categories which constitute ordinary experience have lost their power. The category of substance is lost: solid objects are twisted like ropes; the causal interdependence of things is disregarded: things appear in a complete contingency; temporal sequences are without significance, it does not matter whether an event has happened before or after another event; the spatial dimensions are reduced or dissolved into a horrifying infinity. The organic structures of life are cut into pieces which are arbitrarily (from the biological, not the artistic, point of view) recomposed: limbs are dispersed, colors are separated from their natural carriers. The psychological process (this refers to literature more than to art) is reversed: one lives from the future to the past, and this without rhythm or any kind of meaningful organization. The world of anxiety is a world in which the categories, the structures of reality, have lost their validity. Everybody would be dizzy if causality suddenly ceased to be valid. In Existentialist art (as I like to call it) causality has lost its validity.

Modern art has been attacked as a forerunner of totalitarian systems. The answer that all totalitarian systems have started their careers by attacking modern art is insufficient, for one could say that the totalitarian systems fought modern art just because they tried to resist the meaninglessness expressed in it. The real answer lies deeper. Modern art is not propaganda but revelation. It shows that the reality of our existence is as it is. It does not cover up the reality in which we are living. The question therefore is this: Is the revelation of a situation propaganda for it? If this were the case all art would have to become dishonest beautification. The art propagated by both totalitarianism and democratic conformism is dishonest beautification. It is an idealized naturalism which is preferred because it removes every danger of art becoming critical and revolutionary. The creators of modern art have been able to see the meaninglessness of our existence; they participated in its despair. At the same time they have had the courage to face it and to express it in their pictures and sculptures. They had the courage to be as themselves.

THE COURAGE OF DESPAIR IN CONTEMPORARY PHILOSOPHY

Existential philosophy gives the theoretical formulation of what we have found as the courage of despair in art and literature. Heidegger in *Sein und Zeit* (which has its independent philosophical standing whatever Heidegger may say about it in criticism and retraction) describes the courage of despair in philosophically exact terms. He carefully elaborates the concepts of nonbeing, finitude, anxiety, care, having to die, guilt, conscience, self, participation, and so on. After this he analyses a phenomenon which he calls "resolve." The German word for it, *Entschlossenheit*, points to the symbol of unlocking what anxiety, subjection to conformity, and self-seclusion have locked. Once it is unlocked, one can act, but not according to norms given by anybody or anything. Nobody can give directions for the actions of the "resolute" individual—no God, no conventions, no laws of reason, no norms or principles. *We* must be ourselves, *we* must decide where to go. Our conscience is the call to ourselves. It does not tell anything concrete, it is neither the voice of God nor the awareness of eternal principles. It calls us to ourselves out of the behavior of the average man, out of daily talk, the daily routine, out or the adjustment which is the main principle of the conformist courage to be as a part. But if we follow this call we become inescapably guilty, not through moral weakness but through our existential situation. Having the courage to be as ourselves we become guilty, and we are asked to take this existential guilt upon ourselves. Meaninglessness in all its aspects can be faced only by those who resolutely take the anxiety of finitude and guilt upon themselves. There is no norm, no criterion for what is right and wrong. Resoluteness makes right what shall be right. One of Heidegger's historical functions was to carry through the Existentialist analysis of the courage to be as oneself more fully than anyone else and, historically speaking, more destructively.

Sartre draws consequences from the earlier Heidegger which the later Heidegger did not accept. But it remains doubtful whether Sartre was historically right in drawing these consequences. It was easier for Sartre to draw them than for Heidegger, for in the background of Heidegger's ontology lies the mystical concept of being which is without significance for Sartre. Sartre carried through the consequences of Heidegger's Existentialist analyses without mystical restrictions. This is the reason he has become the symbol of present-day Existentialism, a position which is deserved not so much by the originality of his basic concepts as by the radicalism, consistency, and psychological adequacy with which he has carried them through. I refer above all to his proposition that "the essence of man is his existence." This sentence is like a flash of light which illuminates the whole Existentialist scene. One could call it the most despairing and the most courageous sentence in all Existentialist literature. What it says is that there is no essential nature of man, except in the one point that he can make of himself what he wants. Man creates what he is. Nothing is given to him to determine his creativity. The essence of his being—the "should-be," "the ought-to-be,"—is not something which he finds; he makes it. Man is what he makes of himself. And the courage to be as oneself is the courage to make of oneself what one wants to be.

There are Existentialists of a less radical point of view. Karl Jaspers recommends a new conformity in terms of an all-embracing "philosophical faith"; others speak of a *philosophia perennis;* while Gabriel Marcel moves from an Existentialist radicalism to a position based on the semi-collectivism of medieval thought. Existentialism in philosophy is represented more by Heidegger and Sartre than by anybody else.

THE COURAGE OF DESPAIR IN THE NON-CREATIVE EXISTENTIALIST ATTITUDE

I have dealt in the last sections with people whose creative courage enables them to express existential despair. Not many people are creative. But there is a noncreative Existentialist attitude called cynicism. A cynic today is not the same person the Greeks meant by the term. For the Greeks the cynic was a critic of contemporary culture on the basis of reason and natural law; he was a revolutionary rationalist, a follower of Socrates. Modern cynics are not ready to follow anybody. They have no belief in reason, no criterion of truth, no set of values, no answer to the question of meaning. They try to undermine every norm put before them. Their courage is expressed not creatively but in their form of life. They courageously reject any solution which would deprive them of their freedom of rejecting whatever they want to reject. The cynics are lonely although they need company in order to show their loneliness. They are empty of both preliminary meanings and an ultimate meaning, and therefore easy victims of neurotic anxiety. Much compulsive self-affirmation and much fanatical self-surrender are expressions of the noncreative courage to be as oneself.

THE LIMITS OF THE COURAGE
TO BE AS ONESELF

This leads to the question of the limits of the courage to be as oneself in its creative as well as its uncreative forms. Courage is self-affirmation "in spite of," and the courage to be as oneself is self-affirmation of the self as itself. But one must ask: What is this self that affirms itself? Radical Existentialism answers: What it makes of itself. This is all it can say, because anything more would restrict the absolute freedom of the self. The self, cut off from participation in its world, is an empty shell, a mere possibility. It must act because it lives, but it must redo every action because acting involves him who acts in that upon which he acts. It gives content and for this reason it restricts his freedom to make of himself what he wants. In classical theology, both Catholic and Protestant, only

God has this prerogative: He is *ā sē* (from himself) or absolute freedom. Nothing is in him which is not by him. Existentialism, on the basis of the message that God is dead, gives man the divine "a-se-ity." Nothing shall be in man which is not by man. But man is finite, he is given to himself as what he is. He has received his being and with it the structure of his being, including the structure of finite freedom. And finite freedom is not aseity. Man can affirm himself only if he affirms not an empty shell, a mere possibility, but the structure of being in which he finds himself before action and nonaction. Finite freedom has a definite structure, and if the self tries to trespass on this structure it ends in the loss of itself. The nonparticipating hero in Sartre's *The Age of Reason* is caught in a net of contingencies, coming partly from the subconscious levels of his own self, partly from the environment from which he cannot withdraw. The assuredly empty self is filled with contents which enslave it just because it does not know or accept them as contents. This is true too of the cynic, as was said before. He cannot escape the forces of his self which may drive him into complete loss of the freedom that he wants to preserve.

This dialectical self-destruction of the radical forms of the courage to be as oneself has happened on a world-wide scale in the totalitarian reaction of the 20th century against the revolutionary Existentialism of the 19th century. The Existentialist protest against dehumanization and objectivation, together with its courage to be as oneself, have turned into the most elaborate and oppressive forms of collectivism that have appeared in history. It is the great tragedy of our time that Marxism, which had been conceived as a movement for the liberation of everyone, has been transformed into a system of enslavement of everyone, even of those who enslave the others. It is hard to imagine the immensity of this tragedy in terms of psychological destruction, especially within the intelligentsia. The courage to be was undermined in innumerable people because it was the courage to be in the sense of the revolutionary movements of the 19th century. When it broke down, these people turned either to the neocollectivist system, in a fanatic-neurotic reaction against the cause of their tragic disappointment, or to a cynical-neurotic indifference to all systems and every content.

It is obvious that similar observations can be made on the transformation of the Nietzschean type of the courage to be as oneself into the Fascist-Nazi forms of neocollectivism. The totalitarian machines which these movements produced embodied almost everything against which the courage to be as oneself stands. They used all possible means in order to make such courage impossible. Although, in distinction to communism, this system fell down, its aftermath is confusion, indifference, cynicism. And this is the soil on which the longing for authority and for a new collectivism grows.

The last two chapters, that on the courage to be as a part and that on the courage to be as oneself, have shown

that the former, if carried through radically, leads to the
loss of the self in collectivism and the latter to the loss of
the world in Existentialism. This brings us to the question
of our last chapter: Is there a courage to be which unites
both forms by transcending them?

Courage is the self-affirmation of being in spite of the fact of nonbeing. It is the act of the individual self in taking the anxiety of nonbeing upon itself by affirming itself either as part of an embracing whole or in its individual selfhood. Courage always includes a risk, it is always threatened by nonbeing, whether the risk of losing oneself and becoming a thing within the whole of things or of losing one's world in an empty self-relatedness. Courage needs the power of being, a power transcending the non-being which is experienced in the anxiety of fate and death, which is present in the anxiety of emptiness and meaninglessness, which is effective in the anxiety of guilt and condemnation. The courage which takes this threefold anxiety into itself must be rooted in a power of being that is greater than the power of oneself and the power of one's world. Neither self-affirmation as a part nor self-affirmation as oneself is beyond the manifold threat of nonbeing. Those who are mentioned as representatives of these forms of courage try to transcend themselves and the world in which they participate in order to find the power of be-ing-itself and a courage to be which is beyond the threat of nonbeing. There are no exceptions to this rule; and this

means that every courage to be has an open or hidden
religious root. For religion is the state of being grasped
by the power of being-itself. In some cases the religious
root is carefully covered, in others it is passionately denied; in some it is deeply hidden and in others superfi-
cially. But it is never completely absent. For everything
that is participates in being-itself, and everybody has some
awareness of this participation, especially in the moments
in which he experiences the threat of nonbeing. This leads
us to a final consideration, the double question: How is the
courage to be rooted in being-itself, and how must we
understand being-itself in the light of the courage to be?
The first question deals with the ground of being as source
of the courage to be, the second with courage to be as key
to the ground of being.

THE POWER OF BEING AS SOURCE
OF THE COURAGE TO BE

THE MYSTICAL EXPERIENCE AND
THE COURAGE TO BE

Since the relation of man to the ground of his being
must be expressed in symbols taken from the structure of
being, the polarity of participation and individualization
determines the special character of this relation as it determines the special character of the courage to be. If participation is dominant, the relation to being-itself has a
mystical character, if individualization prevails the relation to being-itself has a personal character, if both

poles are accepted and transcended the relation to being-itself has the character of faith.

In mysticism the individual self strives for a participation in the ground of being which approaches identification. Our question is not whether this goal can ever be reached by a finite being but whether and how mysticism can be the source of the courage to be. We have referred to the mystical background of Spinoza's system, to his way of deriving the self-affirmation of man from the self-affirmation of the divine substance in which he participates. In a similar way all mystics draw their power of self-affirmation from the experience of the power of being-itself with which they are united. But one may ask, can courage be united with mysticism in any way? It seems that in India, for example, courage is considered the virtue of the *kshatriya* (knight), to be found below the levels of the Brahman or the ascetic saint. Mystical identification transcends the aristocratic virtue of courageous self-sacrifice. It is self-surrender in a higher, more complete, and more radical form. It is the perfect form of self-affirmation. But if this is so, it is courage in the larger though not in the narrower sense of the word. The ascetic and ecstatic mystic affirms his own essential being over against the elements of nonbeing which are present in the finite world, the realm of Maya. It takes tremendous courage to resist the lure of appearances. The power of being which is manifest in such courage is so great that the gods tremble in fear of it. The mystic seeks to penetrate the ground of being, the all-present and all-pervasive power of the Brahman. In doing so he affirms his essential self which is identical with the power of the Brahman, while all those who affirm themselves in the bondage of Maya affirm what is not their true self, be they animals, men, or gods. This elevates the mystic's self-affirmation above the courage as a special virtue possessed by the aristocratic-soldiery. But he is not above courage altogether. That which from the point of view of the finite world appears as self-negation is from the point of view of ultimate being the most perfect self-affirmation, the most radical form of courage.

In the strength of this courage the mystic conquers the anxiety of fate and death. Since being in time and space and under the categories of finitude is ultimately unreal, the vicissitudes arising from it and the final nonbeing ending it are equally unreal. Nonbeing is no threat because finite being is, in the last analysis, nonbeing. Death is the negation of that which is negative and the affirmation of that which is positive. In the same way the anxiety of doubt and meaninglessness is taken into the mystical courage to be. Doubt is directed toward everything that is and that, according to its Maya character, is doubtful. Doubt dissolves the veil of Maya, it undermines the defense of mere opinions against ultimate reality. And this manifestation is not exposed to doubt because it is the presupposition of every act of doubt. Without a consciousness of truth itself doubt of truth would be impossible. The anxiety of meaninglessness is conquered where the ultimate meaning is not something definite but the abyss of every definite meaning. The mystic experiences step after step the lack of meaning in the different levels of reality which he enters, works through, and leaves. As long as he walks ahead on this road the anxieties of guilt and condemnation are also conquered. They are not absent. Guilt can be acquired on every level, partly through a failure to fulfill its intrinsic demands, partly through a failure to proceed beyond the level. But as long as the certainty of final fulfillment is given, the anxiety of guilt does not become anxiety of condemnation. There is automatic punishment according to the law of karma, but there is no condemnation in Asiatic mysticism.

The mystical courage to be lasts as long as the mystical situation. Its limit is the state of emptiness of being and meaning, with its horror and despair, which the mystics have described. In these moments the courage to be is reduced to the acceptance of even this state as a way to prepare through darkness for light, through emptiness for abundance. As long as the absence of the power of being is felt as despair, it is the power of being which makes itself felt through despair. To experience this and to endure it is the courage to be of the mystic in the state of emptiness. Although mysticism in its extreme positive and extreme negative aspects is a comparatively rare event, the basic attitude, the striving for union with ultimate reality, and the corresponding courage to take the nonbeing which is implied in finitude upon oneself are a way of life which is accepted by and has shaped large sections of mankind.

But mysticism is more than a special form of the relation to the ground of being. It is an element of every form of this relation. Since everything that is participates in the power of being, the element of identity on which mysticism is based cannot be absent in any religious experience. There is no self-affirmation of a finite being, and there is no courage to be in which the ground of being and its power of conquering nonbeing is not effective. And the experience of the presence of this power is the mystical element even in the person-to-person encounter with God.

THE DIVINE-HUMAN ENCOUNTER AND THE COURAGE TO BE

The pole of individualization expresses itself in the religious experience as a personal encounter with God. And the courage derived from it is the courage of confidence in the personal reality which is manifest in the religious experience. In contradistinction to the mystical union one can call this relation a personal communion with the source of courage. Although the two types are in contrast they do not exclude each other. For they are united by the polar interdependence of individualization and participation. The courage of confidence has often, especially in Protestantism, been identified with the courage of faith. But this is not adequate, because confidence is only one element in faith. Faith embraces both mystical participation and personal confidence. Most parts of the Bible describe the religious encounter in strongly personalist terms. Biblicism, notably that of the Reformers, follows this emphasis. Luther directed his attack against the objective, quantitative, and impersonal elements in the Roman system. He fought for an immediate person-to-person relationship between God and man. In him the courage of confidence reached its highest point in the history of Christian thought. Every work of Luther, especially in his earlier years, is filled with such courage. Again and again he uses the word *trotz*, "in spite of." In spite of all the negativities which he had experienced, in spite of the anxiety which dominated that period, he derived the power of self-affirmation from his unshakable confidence in God and from the personal encounter with him. According to the expressions of anxiety in his period, the negativity his courage had to conquer were symbolized in the figures of death and the devil. It has rightly been said that Albrecht Dürer's engraving, "Knight, Death, and the Devil," is a classic expression of the spirit of the Lutheran Reformation and—it might be added—of Luther's courage of confidence, of his form of the courage to be. A knight in full armor is riding through a valley, accompanied by the figure of death on one side, the devil on the other. Fearlessly, concentrated, confident he looks ahead. He is alone but he is not lonely. In his solitude he participates in the power which gives him the courage to affirm himself in spite of the presence of the negativities of existence. His courage is certainly not the courage to be as a part. The Reformation broke away from the semicollectivism of the Middle Ages. Lu-

ther's courage of confidence is personal confidence, derived from a person-to-person encounter with God.
Neither popes nor councils could give him this confidence. Therefore he had to reject them just because
they relied on a doctrine which blocked off the courage of
confidence. They sanctioned a system in which the anxiety of death and guilt never was completely conquered.
There were many assurances but no certainty, many sup-
ports for the courage of confidence but no unquestionable
foundation. The collective offered different ways of resisting anxiety but no way in which the individual could
take his anxiety upon himself. He never was certain; he
never could affirm his being with unconditional confidence. For he never could encounter the unconditional
directly with his total being, in an immediate personal
relation. There was, except in mysticism, always mediation through the Church, an indirect and partial meeting
between God and the soul. When the Reformation removed the mediation and opened up a direct, total, and
personal approach to God, a new nonmystical courage
to be was possible. It is manifest in the heroic representatives of fighting Protestantism, in the Calvinist as well as
in the Lutheran Reformation, and in Calvinism even more
conspicuously. It is not the heroism of risking martyrdom,
of resisting the authorities, of transforming the structure
of Church and society, but it is the courage of confidence
which makes these men heroic and which is the basis of
the other expressions of their courage. One could say—
and liberal Protestantism often has said—that the courage

of the Reformers is the beginning of the individualistic type of the courage to be as oneself. But such an interpretation confuses a possible historical effect with the matter itself. In the courage of the Reformers the courage to be as oneself is both affirmed and transcended. In comparison with the mystical form of courageous self-affirmation the Protestant courage of confidence affirms the individual self as an individual self in its encounter with God as person. This radically distinguishes the personalism of the Reformation from all the later forms of individualism and Existentialism. The courage of the Reformers is not the courage to be oneself—as it is not the courage to be as a part. It transcends and unites both of them. For the courage of confidence is not rooted in confidence about oneself. The Reformation pronounces the opposite: one can become confident about one's existence only after ceasing to base one's confidence on oneself. On the other hand the courage of confidence is in no way based on anything finite besides oneself, not even on the Church. It is based on God and solely on God, who is experienced in a unique and personal encounter. The courage of the Reformation transcends both the courage to be as a part and the courage to be as oneself. It is threatened neither by the loss of oneself nor by the loss of one's world.

GUILT AND THE COURAGE TO ACCEPT ACCEPTANCE

In the center of the Protestant courage of confidence stands the courage to accept acceptance in spite of the consciousness of guilt. Luther, and in fact the whole period, experienced the anxiety of guilt and condemnation as the main form of their anxiety. The courage to affirm oneself in spite of this anxiety is the courage which we have called the courage of confidence. It is rooted in the personal, total, and immediate certainty of divine forgiveness. There is belief in forgiveness in all forms of man's courage to be, even in neocollectivism. But there is no interpretation of human existence in which it is so predominant as in genuine Protestantism. And there is no movement in history in which it is equally profound and equally paradoxical. In the Lutheran formula that "he who is unjust is just" (in the view of the divine forgiveness) or in the more modern phrasing that "he who is unacceptable is accepted" the victory over the anxiety of guilt and condemnation is sharply expressed. One could say that the courage to be is the courage to accept oneself as accepted in spite of being unacceptable. One does not need to remind the theologians of the fact that this is the genuine meaning of the Pauline-Lutheran doctrine of "justification by faith" (a doctrine which in its original phrasing has become incomprehensible even for students of theology). But one must remind theologians and ministers that in the fight against the anxiety of guilt by psychotherapy the idea of acceptance has received the attention and gained the significance which in the Reformation period was to be seen in phrases like "forgiveness of sins" or "justification through faith." Accepting acceptance though being unacceptable is the basis for the courage of confidence.

Decisive for this self-affirmation is its being independent of any moral, intellectual, or religious precondition: it is not the good or the wise or the pious who are entitled to the courage to accept acceptance but those who are lacking in all these qualities and are aware of being unacceptable. This, however, does not mean acceptance by oneself as oneself. It is not a justification of one's accidental individuality. It is not the Existentialist courage to be as oneself. It is the paradoxical act in which one is accepted by that which infinitely transcends one's individual self. It is in the experience of the Reformers the acceptance of the unacceptable sinner into judging and transforming communion with God.

The courage to be in this respect is the courage to accept the forgiveness of sins, not as an abstract assertion but as the fundamental experience in the encounter with God. Self-affirmation in spite of the anxiety of guilt and condemnation presupposes participation in something which transcends the self. In the communion of healing, for example the psychoanalytic situation, the patient participates in the healing power of the helper by whom he is accepted although he feels himself unacceptable. The healer, in this relationship, does not stand for himself as an individual but represents the objective power of acceptance and self-affirmation. This objective power works through the healer in the patient. Of course, it must be embodied in a person who can realize guilt, who can judge, and who can accept in spite of the judgment. Acceptance by something which is less than personal could never overcome personal self-rejection. A wall to which I confess cannot forgive me. No self-acceptance is possible if one is not accepted in a person-to-person relation. But even if one is personally accepted it needs a self-transcending courage to accept this acceptance, it needs the courage of confidence. For being accepted does not mean that guilt is denied. The healing helper who tried to convince his patient that he was not really guilty would do him a great disservice. He would prevent him from taking his guilt into his self-affirmation. He may help him to transform displaced, neurotic guilt feelings into genuine ones which are, so to speak, put on the right place, but he cannot tell him that there is no guilt in him. He accepts the patient into his communion without condemning anything and without covering up anything.

Here, however, is the point where the religious "acceptance as being accepted" transcends medical healing. Religion asks for the ultimate source of the power which heals by accepting the unacceptable, it asks for God. The acceptance by God, his forgiving or justifying act, is the only and ultimate source of a courage to be which is able to take the anxiety of guilt and condemnation into itself. For the ultimate power of self-affirmation can only be the power of being-itself. Everything less than this, one's own or anybody else's finite power of being, cannot overcome the radical, infinite threat of nonbeing which is experienced in the despair of self-condemnation. This is why the courage of confidence, as it is expressed in a man like Luther, emphasizes unceasingly exclusive trust in God and rejects any other foundation for his courage to be, not only as insufficient but as driving him into more guilt and deeper anxiety. The immense liberation brought to the people of the 16th century by the message of the Reformers and the creation of their indomitable courage to accept acceptance was due to the *sola fide* doctrine, namely to the message that the courage of confidence is conditioned not by anything finite but solely by that which is unconditional itself and which we experience as unconditional in a person-to-person encounter.

FATE AND THE COURAGE TO ACCEPT ACCEPTANCE

As the symbolic figures of death and the devil show, the anxiety of this period was not restricted to the anxiety of guilt. It was also an anxiety of death and fate. The astrological ideas of the later ancient world had been revived by the Renaissance and had influenced even those humanists who joined the Reformation. We have already referred to the Neo-Stoic courage, expressed in some Renaissance pictures, where man directs the vessel of his life although it is driven by the winds of fate. Luther faced the anxiety of fate on another level. He experienced the connection between the anxiety of guilt and the anxiety of fate. It is the uneasy conscience which produces innumerable irrational fears in daily life. The rustling of a dry leaf horrifies him who is plagued by guilt. Therefore conquest of the anxiety of guilt is also conquest of the anxiety of fate. The courage of confidence takes the anxiety of fate as well as the anxiety of guilt into itself. It says "in spite of" to both of them. This is the genuine meaning of the doctrine of providence. Providence is not a theory about some activities of God; it is the religious symbol of the courage of confidence with respect to fate and death. For the courage of confidence says "in spite of" even to death.

Like Paul, Luther was well aware of the connection of the anxiety of guilt with the anxiety of death. In Stoicism and Neo-Stoicism the essential self is not threatened by death, because it belongs to being-itself and transcends nonbeing. Socrates, who in the power of his essential self conquered the anxiety of death, has become the symbol for the courage to take death upon oneself. This is the true meaning of Plato's so-called doctrine of immortality of the soul. In discussing this doctrine we should neglect the arguments for immortality, even those in Plato's *Phaedon,* and concentrate on the image of the dying Socrates. All the arguments, skeptically treated by Plato himself, are attempts to interpret the courage of Socrates, the courage to take one's death into one's self-affirmation. Socrates is certain that the self which the executioners will destroy is not the self which affirms itself in his courage to be. He does not say much about the relation of the two selves, and he could not because they are not numerically two, but one in two aspects. But he makes it clear that the courage to die is the test of the courage to be. A self-affirmation which omits taking the affirmation of one's death into itself tries to escape the test of courage, the facing of nonbeing in the most radical way.

The popular belief in immortality which in the Western world has largely replaced the Christian symbol of resurrection is a mixture of courage and escape. It tries to maintain one's self-affirmation even in the face of one's having to die. But it does this by continuing one's finitude, that is one's having to die, infinitely, so that the actual death never will occur. This, however, is an illusion and, logically speaking, a contradiction in terms. It makes endless what, by definition, must come to an end. The "immortality of the soul" is a poor symbol for the courage to be in the face of one's having to die.

The courage of Socrates (in Plato's picture) was based not on a doctrine of the immortality of the soul but on the affirmation of himself in his essential, indestructible being. He knows that he belongs to two orders of reality and that the one order is transtemporal. It was the courage of Socrates which more than any philosophical reflection revealed to the ancient world that everyone belongs to two orders.

But there was one presupposition in the Socratic (Stoic and Neo-Stoic) courage to take death upon oneself, namely the ability of every individual to participate in both orders, the temporal and the eternal. This presupposition is not accepted by Christianity. According to Christianity we are estranged from our essential being. We are not free to realize our essential being, we are bound to contradict it. Therefore death can be accepted only through a state of confidence in which death has ceased to be the "wages of sin." This, however, is the state of being accepted in spite of being unacceptable. Here is the point in which the ancient world was transformed by Christianity and in which Luther's courage to face death was rooted. It is the being accepted into communion with God that underlies this courage, not a questionable theory of immortality. The encounter with God in Luther is not merely the basis for the courage to take upon oneself sin and condemnation, it is also the basis for taking upon oneself fate and death. For encountering God means encountering transcendent security and transcendent eternity. He who participates in God participates in eternity. But in order to participate in him you must be accepted by him and you must have accepted his acceptance of you.

Luther had experiences which he describes as attacks of utter despair (*Anfechtung*), as the frightful threat of a complete meaninglessness. He felt these moments as satanic attacks in which everything was menaced: his Christian faith, the confidence in his work, the Reformation, the forgiveness of sins. Everything broke down in the extreme moments of this despair, nothing was left of the courage to be. Luther in these moments, and in the descriptions he gives of them, anticipated the descriptions of them by modern Existentialism. But for him this was not the last word. The last word was the first commandment, the statement that God is God. It reminded him of the unconditional element in human experience of which one can be aware even in the abyss of meaninglessness. And this awareness saved him.

It should not be forgotten that the great adversary of Luther, Thomas Münzer, the Anabaptist and religious socialist, describes similar experiences. He speaks of the ultimate situation in which everything finite reveals its finitude, in which the finite has come to its end, in which anxiety grips the heart and all previous meanings fall apart, and in which just for this reason the Divine Spirit can make itself felt and can turn the whole situation into a courage to be whose expression is revolutionary action. While Luther represents ecclesiastical Protestantism, Münzer represents evangelical radicalism. Both men have shaped history, and actually Münzer's views had even more influence in America than Luther's. Both men experienced the anxiety of meaninglessness and described it in terms which had been created by Christian mystics. But in doing so they transcended the courage of confidence which is based on a personal encounter with God. They had to receive elements from the courage to be which is based on mystical union. This leads to a last question: whether the two types of the courage to accept acceptance can be united in view of the all-pervasive presence of the anxiety of doubt and meaninglessness in our own period.

ABSOLUTE FAITH AND THE COURAGE TO BE

We have avoided the concept of faith in our description of the courage to be which is based on mystical union with the ground of being as well as in our description of the courage to be which is based on the personal encounter with God. This is partly because the concept of faith has lost its genuine meaning and has received the connotation of "belief in something unbelievable." But this is not the only reason for the use of terms other than faith. The decisive reason is that I do not think either mystical union or personal encounter fulfills the idea of faith. Certainly there is faith in the elevation of the soul above the finite to the infinite, leading to its union with the ground of being. But more than this is included in the concept of faith. And there is faith in the personal encounter with the personal God. But more than this is included in the concept of faith. Faith is the state of being grasped by the power of being-itself. The courage to be is an expression of faith and what "faith" means must be understood through the courage to be. We have defined courage as the self-affirmation of being in spite of non-being. The power of this self-affirmation is the power of being which is effective in every act of courage. Faith is the experience of this power.

But it is an experience which has a paradoxical character, the character of accepting acceptance. Being-itself transcends every finite being infinitely; God in the divine-human encounter transcends man unconditionally. Faith bridges this infinite gap by accepting the fact that in spite of it the power of being is present, that he who is separated is accepted. Faith accepts "in spite of"; and out of the "in spite of" of faith the "in spite of" of courage is born. Faith is not a theoretical affirmation of something uncertain, it is the existential acceptance of something transcending ordinary experience. Faith is not an opinion but a state. It is the state of being grasped by the power of being which transcends everything that is and in which everything that is participates. He who is grasped by this power is able to affirm himself because he knows that he is affirmed by the power of being-itself. In this point mystical experience and personal encounter are identical. In both of them faith is the basis of the courage to be.

This is decisive for a period in which, as in our own, the anxiety of doubt and meaninglessness is dominant. Certainly the anxiety of fate and death is not lacking in our time. The anxiety of fate has increased with the degree to which the schizophrenic split of our world has removed the last remnants of former security. And the anxiety of guilt and condemnation is not lacking either. It is surprising how much anxiety of guilt comes to the surface in psychoanalysis and personal counseling. The centuries of puritan and bourgeois repression of vital strivings have produced almost as many guilt feelings as the preaching of hell and purgatory in the Middle Ages.

But in spite of these restricting considerations one must say that the anxiety which determines our period is the anxiety of doubt and meaninglessness. One is afraid of having lost or of having to lose the meaning of one's existence. The expression of this situation is the Existentialism of today.

Which courage is able to take nonbeing into itself in

the form of doubt and meaninglessness? This is the most important and most disturbing question in the quest for the courage to be. For the anxiety of meaninglessness undermines what is still unshaken in the anxiety of fate and death and of guilt and condemnation. In the anxiety of guilt and condemnation doubt has not yet undermined the certainty of an ultimate responsibility. We are threatened but we are not destroyed. If, however, doubt and meaninglessness prevail one experiences an abyss in which the meaning of life and the truth of ultimate responsibility disappear. Both the Stoic who conquers the anxiety of fate with the Socratic courage of wisdom and the Christian who conquers the anxiety of guilt with the Protestant courage of accepting forgiveness are in a different situation. Even in the despair of having to die and the despair of self-condemnation meaning is affirmed and certitude preserved. But in the despair of doubt and meaninglessness both are swallowed by nonbeing.

The question then is this: Is there a courage which can conquer the anxiety of meaninglessness and doubt? Or in other words, can the faith which accepts acceptance resist the power of nonbeing in its most radical form? Can faith resist meaninglessness? Is there a kind of faith which can exist together with doubt and meaninglessness? These questions lead to the last aspect of the problem discussed in these lectures and the one most relevant to our time: How is the courage to be possible if all the ways to create it are barred by the experience of their ultimate insufficiency? If life is as meaningless as death, if guilt is as questionable as perfection, if being is no more meaningful than nonbeing, on what can one base the courage to be?

There is an inclination in some Existentialists to answer these questions by a leap from doubt to dogmatic certitude, from meaninglessness to a set of symbols in which the meaning of a special ecclesiastical or political group is embodied. This leap can be interpreted in different ways. It may be the expression of a desire for safety; it may be as arbitrary as, according to Existentialist principles, every decision is; it may be the feeling that the Christian message is the answer to the questions raised by an analysis of human existence; it may be a genuine conversion, independent of the theoretical situation. In any case it is not a solution of the problem of radical doubt. It gives the courage to be to those who are converted but it does not answer the question as to how such a courage is possible in itself. The answer must accept, as its precondition, the state of meaninglessness. It is not an answer if it demands the removal of this state; for that is just what cannot be done. He who is in the grip of doubt and meaninglessness cannot liberate himself from this grip; but he asks for an answer which is valid within and not outside the situation of his despair. He asks for the ultimate foundation of what we have called the "courage of despair." There is only one possible answer, if one does not try to escape the question: namely that the acceptance of despair is in itself faith and on the boundary line of the courage to be. In this situation the meaning of life is reduced to despair about the meaning of life. But as long as this despair is an act of life it is positive in its negativity. Cynically speaking, one could say that it is true to life to be cynical about it. Religiously speaking, one would say that one accepts oneself as accepted in spite of one's despair about the meaning of this acceptance. The paradox of every radical negativity, as long as it is an active negativity, is that it must affirm itself in order to be able to negate itself. No actual negation can be without an implicit affirmation. The hidden pleasure produced by despair witnesses to the paradoxical character of self-negation. The negative lives from the positive it negates.

The faith which makes the courage of despair possible is the acceptance of the power of being, even in the grip of nonbeing. Even in the despair about meaning being affirms itself through us. The act of accepting meaninglessness is in itself a meaningful act. It is an act of faith. We have seen that he who has the courage to affirm his being in spite of fate and guilt has not removed them. He remains threatened and hit by them. But he accepts his acceptance by the power of being-itself in which he participates and which gives him the courage to take the anxieties of fate and guilt upon himself. The same is true of doubt and meaninglessness. The faith which creates the courage to take them into itself has no special content. It is simply faith, undirected, absolute. It is undefinable, since everything defined is dissolved by doubt and meaninglessness. Nevertheless, even absolute faith is not an eruption of subjective emotions or a mood without objective foundation.

An analysis of the nature of absolute faith reveals the following elements in it. The first is the experience of the power of being which is present even in face of the most radical manifestation of nonbeing. If one says that in this experience vitality resists despair one must add that vitality in man is proportional to intentionality. The vitality that can stand the abyss of meaninglessness is aware of a hidden meaning within the destruction of meaning. The second element in absolute faith is the dependence of the experience of nonbeing on the experience of being and the dependence of the experience of meaninglessness on the experience of meaning. Even in the state of despair one has enough being to make despair possible. There is a third element in absolute faith, the acceptance of being accepted. Of course, in the state of despair there is nobody and nothing that accepts. But there is the power of acceptance itself which is experienced. Meaninglessness, as long as it is experienced, includes an experience of the "power of acceptance." To accept this power of acceptance consciously is the religious answer of absolute faith, of a faith which has been deprived by doubt of any concrete content, which nevertheless is faith and the source of the most paradoxical manifestation of the courage to be.

This faith transcends both the mystical experience and the divine-human encounter. The mystical experience seems to be nearer to absolute faith but it is not. Absolute faith includes an element of skepticism which one cannot find in the mystical experience. Certainly mysticism also transcends all specific contents, but not because it doubts them or has found them meaningless; rather it deems them to be preliminary. Mysticism uses the specific contents as grades, stepping on them after having used them. The experience of meaninglessness, however, denies them (and everything that goes with them) without having used them. The experience of meaninglessness is more radical than mysticism. Therefore it transcends the mystical experience.

Absolute faith also transcends the divine-human encounter. In this encounter the subject-object scheme is valid: a definite subject (man) meets a definite object (God). One can reverse this statement and say that a definite subject (God) meets a definite object (man). But in both cases the attack of doubt undercuts the subject-object structure. The theologians who speak so strongly and with such self-certainty about the divine-human encounter should be aware of a situation in which this encounter is prevented by radical doubt and nothing is left but absolute faith. The acceptance of such a situation as religiously valid has, however, the consequence that the concrete contents of ordinary faith must be subjected to criticism and transformation. The courage to be in its radical form is a key to an idea of God which transcends both mysticism and the person-to-person encounter.

THE COURAGE TO BE AS THE KEY TO BEING-ITSELF

NONBEING OPENING UP BEING

The courage to be in all its forms has, by itself, revelatory character. It shows the nature of being, it shows that the self-affirmation of being is an affirmation that over-comes negation. In a metaphorical statement (and every assertion about being-itself is either metaphorical or sym-bolic) one could say that being includes nonbeing but nonbeing does not prevail against it. "Including" is a spa-tial metaphor which indicates that being embraces itself and that which is opposed to it, nonbeing. Nonbeing be-longs to being, it cannot be separated from it. We could not even think "being" without a double negation: being must be thought as the negation of the negation of being. This is why we describe being best by the metaphor "power of being." Power is the possibility a being has to actualize itself against the resistance of other beings. If we speak of the power of being-itself we indicate that being affirms itself against nonbeing. In our discussion of courage and life we have mentioned the dynamic under-standing of reality by the philosophers of life. Such an understanding is possible only if one accepts the view that nonbeing belongs to being, that being could not be the ground of life without nonbeing. The self-affirmation of being without nonbeing would not even be self-affirma-tion but an immovable self-identity. Nothing would be manifest, nothing expressed, nothing revealed. But non-being drives being out of its seclusion, it forces it to affirm itself dynamically. Philosophy has dealt with the dynamic self-affirmation of being-itself wherever it spoke dialecti-cally, notably in Neoplatonism, Hegel, and the philoso-phers of life and process. Theology has done the same whenever it took the idea of the living God seriously, most obviously in the trinitarian symbolization of the inner life of God. Spinoza, in spite of his static definition of substance (which is his name for the ultimate power of being), unites philosophical and mystical tendencies when he speaks of the love and knowledge with which God loves and knows himself through the love and knowledge of finite beings. Nonbeing (that in God which makes his self-affirmation dynamic) opens up the divine self-seclusion and reveals him as power and love. Nonbeing makes God a living God. Without the No he has to overcome in himself and in his creature, the divine Yes to himself would be lifeless. There would be no revelation of the ground of being, there would be no life.

But where there is nonbeing there is finitude and anxiety. If we say that nonbeing belongs to being-itself, we say that finitude and anxiety belong to being-itself. Wherever philosophers or theologians have spoken of the divine blessedness they have implicitly (and sometimes explicitly) spoken of the anxiety of finitude which is eternally taken into the blessedness of the divine infinity. The infinite embraces itself and the finite, the Yes includes itself and the No which it takes into itself, blessedness comprises itself and the anxiety of which it is the conquest. All this is implied if one says that being includes nonbeing and that through nonbeing it reveals itself. It is a highly symbolic language which must be used at this point. But its symbolic character does not diminish its truth; on the contrary, it is a condition of its truth. To speak unsymbolically about being-itself is untrue.

The divine self-affirmation is the power that makes the

self-affirmation of the finite being, the courage to be, possible. Only because being-itself has the character of self-affirmation inspite of nonbeing is courage possible. Courage participates in the self-affirmation of being-itself, it participates in the power of being which prevails against nonbeing. He who receives this power in an act of mystical or personal or absolute faith is aware of the source of his courage to be.

Man is not necessarily aware of this source. In situations of cynicism and indifference he is not aware of it. But it works in him as long as he maintains the courage to take his anxiety upon himself. In the act of the courage to be the power of being is effective in us, whether we recognize it or not. Every act of courage is a manifestation of the ground of being, however questionable the content of the act may be. The content may hide or distort true being, the courage in it reveals true being. Not arguments but the courage to be reveals the true nature of being-itself. By affirming our being we participate in the self-affirmation of being-itself. There are no valid arguments for the "existence" of God, but there are acts of courage in which we affirm the power of being, whether we know it or not. If we know it, we accept acceptance consciously. If we do not know it, we nevertheless accept it and participate in it. And in our acceptance of that which we do not know the power of being is manifest to us. Courage has revealing power, the courage to be is the key to being-itself.

THEISM TRANSCENDED

The courage to take meaninglessness into itself presupposes a relation to the ground of being which we have called "absolute faith." It is without a *special* content, yet it is not without content. The content of absolute faith is the "God above God." Absolute faith and its consequence, the courage that takes the radical doubt, the doubt about God, into itself, transcends the theistic idea of God.

Theism can mean the unspecified affirmation of God. Theism in this sense does not say what it means if it uses the name of God. Because of the traditional and psychological connotations of the word God such an empty theism can produce a reverent mood if it speaks of God. Politicians, dictators, and other people who wish to use rhetoric to make an impression on their audience like to use the word God in this sense. It produces the feeling in their listeners that the speaker is serious and morally trustworthy. This is especially successful if they can brand their foes as atheistic. On a higher level people without a definite religious commitment like to call themselves theistic, not for special purposes but because they cannot stand a world without God, whatever this God may be. They need some of the connotations of the word God and they are afraid of what they call atheism. On the highest level of this kind of theism the name of God is used as a poetic or practical symbol, expressing a profound emotional state or the highest ethical idea. It is a theism which stands on the boundary line between the second type of theism and what we call "theism transcended." But it is still too indefinite to cross this boundary line. The atheistic negation of this whole type of theism is as vague as the theism itself. It may produce an irreverent mood and angry reaction of those who take their theistic affirmation seriously. It may even be felt as justified against the rhetorical-political abuse of the name God, but it is ultimately as irrelevant as the theism which it negates. It cannot reach the state of despair any more than the theism against which it fights can reach the state of faith.

Theism can have another meaning, quite contrary to the first one: it can be the name of what we have called the divine-human encounter. In this case it points to those elements in the Jewish-Christian tradition which emphasize the person-to-person relationship with God. Theism in this sense emphasizes the personalistic passages in the Bible and the Protestant creeds, the personalistic image of God, the word as the tool of creation and revelation, the ethical and social character of the kingdom of God, the personal nature of human faith and divine forgiveness, the historical vision of the universe, the idea of a divine purpose, the infinite distance between creator and creature, the absolute separation between God and the world, the conflict between holy God and sinful man, the person-to-person character of prayer and practical devotion. Theism in this sense is the nonmystical side of biblical religion and historical Christianity. Atheism from the point of view of this theism is the human attempt to escape the

divine-human encounter. It is an existential—not a theoretical—problem.

Theism has a third meaning, a strictly theological one.
Theological theism is, like every theology, dependent on
the religious substance which it conceptualizes. It is dependent on theism in the first sense insofar as it tries to
prove the necessity of affirming God in some way; it
usually develops the so-called arguments for the "existence" of God. But it is more dependent on theism in the
second sense insofar as it tries to establish a doctrine of
God which transforms the person-to-person encounter
with God into a doctrine about two persons who may or
may not meet but who have a reality independent of each
other.

Now theism in the first sense must be transcended because it is irrelevant, and theism in the second sense must
be transcended because it is one-sided. But theism in the
third sense must be transcended because it is wrong. It is
bad theology. This can be shown by a more penetrating
analysis. The God of theological theism is a being beside
others and as such a part of the whole of reality. He certainly is considered its most important part, but as a part
and therefore as subjected to the structure of the whole.
He is supposed to be beyond the ontological elements and
categories which constitute reality. But every statement
subjects him to them. He is seen as a self which has a
world, as an ego which is related to a thou, as a cause
which is separated from its effect, as having a definite
space and an endless time. He is a being, not being-itself.

As such he is bound to the subject-object structure of reality, he is an object for us as subjects. At the same time we are objects for him as a subject. And this is decisive for the necessity of transcending theological theism. For God as a subject makes me into an object which is nothing more than an object. He deprives me of my subjectivity because he is all-powerful and all-knowing. I revolt and try to make *him* into an object, but the revolt fails and becomes desperate. God appears as the invincible tyrant, the being in contrast with whom all other beings are without freedom and subjectivity. He is equated with the recent tyrants who with the help of terror try to transform everything into a mere object, a thing among things, a cog in the machine they control. He becomes the model of everything against which Existentialism revolted. This is the God Nietzsche said had to be killed because nobody can tolerate being made into a mere object of absolute knowledge and absolute control. This is the deepest root of atheism. It is an atheism which is justified as the reaction against theological theism and its disturbing implications. It is also the deepest root of the Existentialist despair and the widespread anxiety of meaninglessness in our period.

Theism in all its forms is transcended in the experience we have called absolute faith. It is the accepting of the acceptance without somebody or something that accepts. It is the power of being-itself that accepts and gives the courage to be. This is the highest point to which our analysis has brought us. It cannot be described in the way the

God of all forms of theism can be described. It cannot be described in mystical terms either. It transcends both mysticism and personal encounter, as it transcends both the courage to be as a part and the courage to be as oneself.

THE GOD ABOVE GOD AND THE COURAGE TO BE

The ultimate source of the courage to be is the "God above God"; this is the result of our demand to transcend theism. Only if the God of theism is transcended can the anxiety of doubt and meaninglessness be taken into the courage to be. The God above God is the object of all mystical longing, but mysticism also must be transcended in order to reach him. Mysticism does not take seriously the concrete and the doubt concerning the concrete. It plunges directly into the ground of being and meaning, and leaves the concrete, the world of finite values and meanings, behind. Therefore it does not solve the problem of meaninglessness. In terms of the present religious situation this means that Eastern mysticism is not the solution of the problems of Western Existentialism, although many people attempt this solution. The God above the God of theism is not the devaluation of the meanings which doubt has thrown into the abyss of meaninglessness; he is their potential restitution. Nevertheless absolute faith agrees with the faith implied in mysticism in that both transcend the theistic objectivation of a God who is a being. For mysticism such a God is not more real than any finite being, for the courage to be such a God has disappeared in the abyss of meaninglessness with every other value and meaning.

The God above the God of theism is present, although hidden, in every divine-human encounter. Biblical religion as well as Protestant theology are aware of the paradoxical character of this encounter. They are aware that if God encounters man God is neither object nor subject and is therefore above the scheme into which theism has forced him. They are aware that personalism with respect to God is balanced by a transpersonal presence of the divine. They are aware that forgiveness can be accepted only if the power of acceptance is effective in man— biblically speaking, if the power of grace is effective in man. They are aware of the paradoxical character of every prayer, of speaking to somebody to whom you cannot speak because he is not "somebody," of asking somebody of whom you cannot ask anything because he gives or gives not before you ask, of saying "thou" to somebody who is nearer to the I than the I is to itself. Each of these paradoxes drives the religious consciousness toward a God above the God of theism.

The courage to be which is rooted in the experience of the God above the God of theism unites and transcends the courage to be as a part and the courage to be as oneself. It avoids both the loss of oneself by participation and the loss of one's world by individualization. The acceptance of the God above the God of theism makes us a part of that which is not also a part but is the ground of the whole.

Therefore our self is not lost in a larger whole, which submerges it in the life of a limited group. If the self participates in the power of being-itself it receives itself back. For the power of being acts through the power of the individual selves. It does not swallow them as every limited whole, every collectivism, and every conformism does. This is why the Church, which stands for the power of being-itself or for the God who transcends the God of the religions, claims to be the mediator of the courage to be. A church which is based on the authority of the God of theism cannot make such a claim. It inescapably develops into a collectivist or semicollectivist system itself.

But a church which raises itself in its message and its devotion to the God above the God of theism without sacrificing its concrete symbols can mediate a courage which takes doubt and meaninglessness into itself. It is the Church under the Cross which alone can do this, the Church which preaches the Crucified who cried to God who remained his God after the God of confidence had left him in the darkness of doubt and meaninglessness. To be as a part in such a church is to receive a courage to be in which one cannot lose one's self and in which one receives one's world.

Absolute faith, or the state of being grasped by the God beyond God, is not a state which appears beside other states of the mind. It never is something separated and definite, an event which could be isolated and described. It is always a movement in, with, and under other states of the mind. It is the situation on the boundary of man's possibilities. It *is* this boundary. Therefore it is both the courage of despair and the courage in and above every courage. It is not a place where one can live, it is without the safety of words and concepts, it is without a name, a church, a cult, a theology. But it is moving in the depth of all of them. It is the power of being, in which they participate and of which they are fragmentary expressions.

One can become aware of it in the anxiety of fate and death when the traditional symbols, which enable men to stand the vicissitudes of fate and the horror of death have lost their power. When "providence" has become a superstition and "immortality" something imaginary that which once was the power in these symbols can still be present and create the courage to be in spite of the experience of a chaotic world and a finite existence. The Stoic courage returns but not as the faith in universal reason. It returns as the absolute faith which says Yes to being without seeing anything concrete which could conquer the nonbeing in fate and death.

And one can become aware of the God above the God of theism in the anxiety of guilt and condemnation when the traditional symbols that enable men to withstand the anxiety of guilt and condemnation have lost their power. When "divine judgment" is interpreted as a psychological complex and forgiveness as a remnant of the "father-image," what once was the power in those symbols can still be present and create the courage to be in spite of the experience of an infinite gap between what we are and what we ought to be. The Lutheran courage returns but not supported by the faith in a judging and forgiving God. It returns in terms of the absolute faith which says Yes although there is no special power that conquers guilt. The courage to take the anxiety of meaninglessness upon oneself is the boundary line up to which the courage to be can go. Beyond it is mere non-being. Within it all forms of courage are re-established in the power of the God above the God of theism. *The courage to be is rooted in the God who appears when God has disappeared in the anxiety of doubt.*

INDEX